KISS AND TELL

KISS AND TELL

Make Love The Married Way

Virgil L. Brady

iUniverse, Inc.
Bloomington

Kiss and Tell
Make Love The Married Way

iUniverse books may be ordered through booksellers or by contacting:

iUniverse
1663 Liberty Drive
Bloomington, IN 47403
www.iuniverse.com
1-800-Authors (1-800-288-4677)

ISBN: 978-1-4620-5934-8 (sc)
ISBN: 978-1-4620-5935-5 (ebk)

Printed in the United States of America

iUniverse rev. date: 10/18/2011

TABLE OF CONTENTS

Introduction

Marriage is difficult. For me this is a positive statement and not a negative. Acknowledging that marriage is difficult has been an important step for making our married love what we want it to be.

My wonderful wife, Elaine, and I are just like every other couple with our own set of problems. At times the storms have been so intense that neither of us was sure our marriage would withstand the pressure.

However, we endured and eventually thrived after realizing there are ways to repair the damage, heal the hurts and navigate ourselves back onto the road towards a healthy marriage. It didn't happen overnight, and redefining our relationship took a lot of wise counsel and re-evaluation by both of us.

Sunday evening was the time when we led and attended our marriage support group at the church. In the afternoon Elaine asked me, "What topic are you thinking about presenting to the group tonight?" When I told her my idea she said, "That seems so negative. I'd rather do something that is positive. We seem to dwell too much on the negative." "What, for you, would be a positive topic," I asked. "How about naming three things I like best about you, or why I want to spend the rest of my life with you?"

Elaine and I have had frequent discussions on what constitutes a negative and a positive marriage topic. There are many negative consequences that arise by ignoring an elephant in the room. To acknowledge the elephant and deal with its presence, leads to positive results.

Positive things have happened in our marriage as a result of Elaine and I being forthright in addressing the pivotal issues facing every marriage. This is not to say it has been a cake walk.

I want you and your spouse to work your way through the crazy maze of being a husband and wife and enjoy the richness and intimacy that God intended in the creation of marriage.

My prayer is that your marriage will become stronger and healthier as you KISS (Keep In Shape Systematically) and TELL (communicate, communicate, communicate)

My main purpose is to help couples build a healthy marriage as they identify the numerous and complex issues that are part of every marriage.

A second purpose of this book is to assist local churches in making marriage a central part of their ministry. Both laity and pastors talk about the importance of family values, yet only a small percentage of local churches have made marriage issues a major part of their programs, groups, classes or sermons. This book will provide a user-friendly resource for laity and pastors in initiating marriage support groups and workshops.

A word of special thanks to my wife, Elaine. Her committed love, effervescence and gratitude for life has inspired my understanding of what makes a healthy marriage. Indeed, she is my co-author.

I am indebted to Jenny Brown who took my original text and made it, what my wife termed, "more interesting." This is the third book Margaret and Harold Jones have proof read. I have appreciated their wisdom and support.

1

Learning to Kiss and Tell

When my wife, Elaine, and I had been married about ten years, we made a drastic decision. We decided to spend more time making love.

No, Elaine didn't take some sex quiz in Cosmo and no, I didn't have a mid-life crisis. We just realized that in the past decade we hadn't spent much time "making love." Don't get me wrong, we had been having sex, but we weren't making love.

This one decision forever changed the landscape of our marriage.

The whole idea came to us as a gift from another couple who we knew through church. One day they called and asked if they could set up a time to come by our house to drop off a gift. We settled on the next evening as a good time to get together.

When the couple arrived, we all sat down in the living room and made small talk about our children and our church. I'd been curious about the gift the man had mentioned on the phone; but when they came in, neither the husband nor wife carried a present.

My curiosity got the best of me; and after a while, I had to ask.

Turned out, the gift was a weekend at a marriage seminar. As their pastor, I was a little taken back. I wondered if they had overheard one of our "heated" discussions or picked up on one of our power struggles.

"I didn't know you knew how bad our marriage was," I quickly joked.

But the couple said they admired our marriage and that the seminars were for couples who had good marriages, but could use a tune-up.

We had no idea how bad we were in need of a tune-up until we arrived at the Marriage Encounter weekend.

It was while at the conference that we decided to spend more time making love. For the most part, we had been happy those early years because we were "in love." But we weren't diving in and examining the depth that is involved in marriage issues. Instead, we were skimming the surface and ignoring significant issues that were lurking and waiting to rear their ugly heads in rocky times.

We suddenly saw that we were taking each other for granted, not addressing issues in our marriage and being lackadaisical about our relationship. Elaine and I were hit with the reality that if we allowed ourselves to stay on the same path of complacency, our marriage would continue to deteriorate and probably crumble. We realized we had not laid a strong foundation for our marriage.

We were not experiencing marriage as God intended it. We were not making love like God intended it either. Instead, we were busy having children, establishing our careers and operating on our feelings.

With the guidance of the leaders that weekend, we took a deeper look at how making love could solidify the foundation of our marriage.

Couples often find themselves in a marital mess and wonder how in the world they got to such a place. What happened to the person they "dove" into love with? We sometimes forget that romantic love cannot sustain us through life's ups and downs. I use the word "dove" versus "fall" in love because I believe we do and can have control over how and whom we love—if we so choose.

Did you ever notice that the marriage vows we all regurgitated at the altar don't include any verbiage about how we feel? That's because feelings won't always lead us to do what is needed to make love grow and flourish. Instead, when we decide to repeat our vows, we are committing to make an effort to love even when our feelings toward our partner aren't warm and fuzzy.

In the dictionary, the word "make" is defined as: to build, form, shape, craft, formulate, generate, fashion, express, convey, form, put together, bring about, cause to be or become or construct.

After seeing how the word "make" is defined, it is somewhat presumptuous to say we make love. We cannot make something that already exists. Love is a gift that is given to us by God. It is then up to us to decide how we are going to build, form, shape, craft and express the gift that we have received.

Think about it this way. When we say things like "I'm going to make a cake," are we really making a cake or are we using ingredients and building a cake?

It's just like "baking" a healthy marriage. We can take the gifts God offers to us and build a marriage like God intended. On the flip side, we can also leave out essential ingredients; and we'll have a tasteless, bland relationship where communication problems abound and our feelings dictate our behavior.

There are two essential ingredients for crafting, shaping, and building a firm foundation for a healthy marriage. These two rules must be put into place in order to fashion the kind of commitment we want and God intended when each of us was given the gift of love.

I. Decide to be intentional and systematic about spending more time making love.

By this I mean take time to build love for your spouse, even when you don't feel like it. Learn to understand the issues that are hampering your marriage. But remember, knowledge alone isn't enough; you must work through the issues with your partner.

Healthy marriages intentionally and systematically address issues on a regular basis.

I use an acronym to help remember how to lay the foundation of a healthy marriage. It is **KISS: Keeping In Shape Systematically.** Throughout the book, you will see the **KISS** acronym. It will be used to help you construct your comprehensive plan for keeping your marriage in shape.

As a sports enthusiast, I have seen what it takes to make a successful athlete. When I say successful, I don't mean being better than everyone else, but instead I'm defining it as reaching one's true potential.

It takes practice, and above all, it takes staying in shape. Let's face it; there are days when even the most well-known athletes probably don't feel like working out. But they do it anyway. They intentionally plan their schedules to include exercise. It's the only way to stay strong and on top of their game. Each workout is part of a comprehensive plan.

Regular work-outs and stretching also decrease the risk of injury when it comes to athletics. It by no means eliminates injuries, but it does minimize the athlete's chance of getting hurt.

A marriage needs the same type of protection and plan. Of course, no one feels like putting kindness and patience into practice with their spouse every day; but it is the sure-fire way for your marriage to reach its potential.

A marriage won't be at its best if you sporadically give your love to your husband or wife. It happens when you are vigilant about it even on days when you don't feel like it. In marriages and sports the old adage is often times true: you get out of it what you put into it.

When those difficult times in marriage arise such as extended family intrusions, the loss of a job or home, or the temptation to stray seems so great, your marriage depends on the time you invested in it. Is your marriage in good enough shape to make it through a marathon filled with pain? Are you putting yourself in a position where you can be successful? If the conditioning is there, it will pay off and give you the power to keep your marriage intact when the game is on the line.

Recently, I was watching a basketball game on television. The score was tied at 79 with only a minute to go. The announcer said, "I can see how the long game is getting to some of the players. Some are noticeably tired. Their shots are not falling. They are not moving as quickly. We are about to find out which team is in the best shape during these final seconds." The game rested on who had built up their stamina long before the win was on the line.

Hopefully, your marriage will last a long time. But if we are not systematic about keeping our marriages in shape, we can become tired, weary and disillusioned. There are no short cuts; it takes discipline, sacrifice and an investment in your marriage.

What if a top NBA player told his coach that he just didn't have time to practice? Do you think he'd be a starting player for long? A player would be foolish to think so. The same goes for any couple who says they are too busy to invest in their marriage. It is imperative to spend intentional time and energy on your spouse if you want to build a lasting and healthy marriage. This commitment will not eliminate problems. It will decrease the risk of injuring your marriage to the point of no return.

II. Surround yourself with God's love.

Our love is inconsistent	**God's love is consistent**
Our love is conditional	**God's love is unconditional**
Our love is limited	**God's love is lasting**

Looking at the above comparisons, who wouldn't want the love God offers to flow through their marriage? Our love for one another and for ourselves grows stronger as we connect with the power of God's love, which is freely given to us, even though we do not deserve it. In those moments where our love wavers and is in danger of breaking, the best decision is to connect to the sure, firm foundation of God's unconditional love. This kind of love, which comes to us unearned, affects all aspects of our marriage, including the ones we are sometimes reluctant to talk about.

When Elaine and I were married, we were committed to making God an integral part of our relationship. But, like many couples, we tended to believe that being a good person was the main purpose of religion. We did not fully grasp the power of God's unconditional love. Many people see God as a rule-setter whose main purpose is to give us a list of "thou shalls" and "thou shall nots."

Of course, goodness and morality are very important; but they lack the power for enriching a marriage in the same way as infusing a relationship with the unconditional love of God.

This is especially true in the difficult times of life, when love is not working as we would like. Being a good and moral person does not hold the power we need for dealing with the many and complex issues surrounding marriage.

Bob and Mary had been active members of the church for many years. One Sunday, as we were eating lunch, I said to Elaine, "I haven't seen Bob and Mary in worship for over a month. That is not like them." Elaine responded, "I think they are having some problems in their family. I hear one of their kids got into trouble."

On Monday, I phoned Bob and Mary and asked if I could come by their house and visit. As we sat in their living room, they quickly confirmed what Elaine had heard. Yes, their teenager had been in some serious trouble. Feelings of failure were consuming them. More importantly, they felt people in church would agree they had failed. They were convinced the church people would think they were not good Christians. Their definition of a Christian is someone who is good and moral.

John and I played golf together. We talked about many things, but religion was a topic he avoided. One day he told me, "I am not into organized religion. I am just as good of a person as those who go to church. I don't need church in order to be a good person." I agreed. John was a good person. When it came to morals, his values were consistent with what I understand to be Christian values. John did seem to be somewhat self-satisfied in his goodness, especially when he compared himself to others.

I remember the day I received a phone call from John at my office. He asked if he could come by and visit. I welcomed him into my office. He sat down and began to tell me he was having relationship problems at work, even to the point of jeopardizing his job. Also, he confessed his marriage had gone sour. His wife even mentioned divorce. He was feeling lonely, guilty, afraid and helpless. Being a good and moral person lacked the power he needed in this difficult time of life.

One of the my biggest challenges as a pastor has been to help people like Bob and Mary and John understand that being a Christian is not primarily about being good and moral, but experiencing the power that comes from receiving the Grace, the unconditional love of God.

A few years back, a couple, who I will call Mark and Kit came to me for counseling. I remember them so vividly because of the way they started off the session.

Just after sitting down, one of them blurted out, "We're here because we're having sexual problems." Most couples have trouble approaching this subject with each other, let alone with their pastor.

They both went on to tell me they rarely fought or got mad at each other, but they just weren't sexually attracted to each other anymore. The romance was gone. As they talked, I soon realized they had other problems, not just in bed.

In their 12 years of marriage, they had never been systematic or intentional about keeping their marriage in shape. They had no foundation. Sure, they went to church; but they both talked about God as some force in the universe meant to make people good and moral. They had no idea how God's love could impact their marriage.

Before we could tackle their sexual problems, we had to tackle some bigger issues which would have a positive effect on their attraction issues.

Rarely are sexual problems in two healthy people tied to a physical problem. Instead, issues in the bedroom usually have their roots in the emotional barriers that have been built between a husband and wife.

As they talked in counseling, I soon began to see their stifled view of God left them both with feelings of guilt and fear when it came to having a healthy, active sex life. Neither Kit nor Mark understood that God's essential nature is unconditional love.

This marriage was not grounded on God's unconditional love which made it impossible for them to appreciate God's gift of a full life, including a full sex life. Their eyes had to be opened to looking at God in a whole new light. This truth helped them understand the freedom and joy that comes from experiencing the power of God's unconditional love.

When Kit and Mark made a decision to infiltrate their marriage and love for each other with God's love, it made a world of difference. Like all beneficial marriage improvement techniques, it didn't change their sex lives overnight. It took time for them to discover the unconditional love of God who wants our lives and marriages to be full of happiness and joy.

One of the most intelligent decisions Elaine and I made in our marriage was to infuse our marriage with the love of God. This enabled us to look honestly at ourselves rather than focusing on what our spouse was or was not doing.

Faith is much more than believing there is a God. Faith is saying "yes" to God. Yes, I will seek to understand fully the nature of God's unconditional love. Yes, I will build my marriage on this consistent and lasting love. Yes, I understand that accepting God's love means accepting my spouse as he/she is rather than insisting on blaming or changing.

It is God who makes love. God's unconditional love is a gift. When someone gives us a gift that is neither earned nor deserved, gratitude is the rational response. I have found healthy marriages begin with encircling love with gratitude to God for the gift of life and for God's unconditional love.

I am not implying if you are having problems that you are not experiencing God's love in your life and marriage. I'm sure there are good marriages out there who do not view their love as a gift from God.

Believing in God's Grace and receiving God's love as a gift does not guarantee our problems will be avoided. However, once we build our marriages with the foundation of God's love, we have a divine truth to guide and empower us when we are traveling down those difficult roads.

Elaine and I can testify that faith in God's Grace is a major factor when it comes to growing love from the romantic stages to the more mature married love.

Several months ago I was not feeling well. I had all the symptoms of a bad flu, sore throat, nasal and chest congestion, and low grade fever. It had gone on for over a week and finally I went to see the doctor. After examining me he said, "You have a viral infection. It takes time for this to run its course." "Aren't you going to give me anything?" I asked. "I mean, it has already gone on for over a week. Can't you give me a prescription, a pill? I want something. This is getting old." The doctor responded, "Get plenty of rest, drink lots of liquids, eat healthy and exercise." "But I want . . . ?" The doctor interrupted, "Nope, I can't prescribe anything that will help you. All I can do is invite you to do this process that I have suggested."

There are many times when we are not feeling very well about how the marriage is going. When we conclude it has gone on for too long, we want someone to give us a prescription that will change the situation. If you want a prescription for making a healthy marriage, I suggest you not continue reading this book. For what follows is an invitation into a process that takes time. For Elaine and me it is a process that has continued over our 48 years of marriage. No prescription. No quick, easy fix, but rather a creative, wonderful process.

The doctor suggested that I would get better through rest, drinking plenty of fluids, eating healthy and exercise. Your marriage will become healthier, not through any prescription, but through the life-long process of finding rest and renewal in God's unconditional love (grace), drinking of the water so you will never thirst (John 3:14), eating the food Jesus says does not perish but endures (John 6:27), and exercise (KISS).

Are you ready to begin the process of applying these two essential ingredients to your marriage? Read on as you prepare yourself to KISS and tell with your spouse.

QUESTIONS FOR PERSONAL RELFECTION
AND
DISCUSSION WITH YOUR SPOUSE

KISS 1: If you decided to keep your marriage in shape systematically, what specific steps would you have to take?

KISS 2: If you and your spouse made God's unconditional love and Grace the foundation of your marriage, how would you see it affecting your relationship?

KISS 3: Share with your spouse your experience of receiving God's Grace and the significance that a true understanding of God's unconditional love has on a person versus just being a good and moral person.

2

What Do You Mean, A Healthy Marriage?

I usually open a marriage workshop with the following question: What do you think makes a healthy marriage?

In every audience, it's usually a toss-up between "trust" and "communication." My vote rarely makes the list.

I believe the number one thing that makes a marriage healthy is when spouses love themselves. Sound a bit self-centered? It's not.

Think about it, trusting another person becomes problematical when we do not love ourselves. Communication skills are undermined when we do not love ourselves.

People who love themselves validate their fundamental value. They respect themselves. Many centuries before modern psychology came along with talk of self-esteem and self-love, Jesus talked about the importance of loving self in order to fully love others. (Mark 22:39)

Self-acceptance is the word used by many therapists, theologians and authors of self-help books. Self-acceptance happens when we affirm and love ourselves as we are, including our strengths and weaknesses and our successes and failures.

Some people might react negatively to the word "self-acceptance" simply because it implies resignation and complacency. However, when we truly accept ourselves we will then proceed down the path of becoming more than we are. When we accept ourselves, our failures are seen as opportunities for growth rather than as defeat.

Those who love themselves are more likely to refrain from abusing their bodies. They will exercise. They will put healthy food into their bodies. Those who love themselves will keep their minds alive and growing. Those who love themselves will do all they can to continually activate their spiritual life. Loving yourself will be manifested in gratitude for the gift of your life, body, mind and spirit.

Self-love and self-acceptance have been criticized as leading to self-centeredness. However, true self-love leads away from self-centeredness because it produces a positive self-image and feelings of inner security. If we are to become less self-centered, it will come as we love and accept ourselves.

These are important questions for every married person:

- Do I love myself?
- Do I have good self-esteem?
- Do I see myself as a person of value and worth?
- Am I self-confident and self-assured?

The answers to these questions indicate how secure or insecure you are.

The words secure and insecure have to do with how you feel about yourself as a person, not about your skills or talents. For example, you may be confident in your ability to play a musical instrument, compete in a sport, build a house or run a company. Hopefully, all of us have something about which we feel secure. I feel insecure if called upon to sing a solo in front of two people or if I have to figure out why a car has stopped functioning.

When I speak of being insecure or secure I am referring to our basic self-concept. Do you love yourself, respect and accept yourself? Or is your sense of self-worth weak and fragile? Is your self-worth tied to what other people think of you?

While all of us have both secure and insecure feelings, the vast majority of people in our culture are more insecure than secure. Accepting this truth is basic for making a healthy marriage.

Looking at a list of insecure feelings, just think about how often we experience these feelings. People often feel: worry, unloved, vulnerable, violated, used, unimportant, unappreciated, resentful, rejected, pressured, overwhelmed, nervous, misunderstood, lonely, jealous, insignificant, guilty, frustrated, embarrassed, irritated, disappointed, depressed, confused, ashamed, anxious, afraid, put down, dejected, weak, despair, devastated, out of control, incompetent, inadequate, unsure, helpless, discouraged and fragmented.

After reading that long, but not exhaustive list, don't start thinking you are the most insecure person on the planet. Insecurity is normal and it can become a source of power and love when understood and addressed openly and honestly in a marriage. Some people use the expression "inferiority complex" when they are actually talking about insecurities. Just because we will have some insecurities does not mean we are inferior. It is not inevitable that our insecure feelings produce negative results in a relationship.

When couples come to me for counseling I begin with the question, "Why have you come? Tell me what is going on." Ninety-nine percent of the time the response is predictable. Each spouse begins to define the issue/problem. It does not take very long before it is clear that each is pointing to the other as the source of the problem.

Then I take my turn and point out that the source of the problem has roots in each spouse's feelings of insecurity. The walls immediately go up. I immediately meet resistance. It is so much easier to point out our partner's flaws and insecurities than to acknowledge our own.

Early in my marriage, I wish someone had pointed out how insecure I was and gone on to help me understand how to deal with it. It would have been helpful, although I doubt I would have listened.

If we learn to understand how life experiences contribute to our feelings of insecurity, it can make our self-love increase and, as a result, improve our marriage.

Let's look at some common life experiences that contribute to our insecurities:

1. Insecurities begin at birth as we are cast into this world kicking and screaming. We came from the womb where every need was met. Now we find ourselves in a situation where our needs may or may not be met as we were accustomed to in the womb.

We all adjust but there is always within us the trauma of transitioning from absolute security of the womb to the insecurity of reality. These insecure feelings are basic to our psychological makeup and thus affect our relationship with others who also share the same separation experience of birth.

2. Feelings of insecurity continue to be established throughout our early years, as parents necessarily set expectations and emphasize what is right and wrong. Children learn there are rewards and punishments connected to the expectations. Small children feel they will be loved if and when they do what is expected.

The uncertainty of how, when and if they might receive their parent's disapproval promotes the inevitable feelings of insecurity. It is an interesting paradox. Children need to be taught right and wrong. Consequences are an important part of the learning process. Without rules, expectations and consequences children would feel even more insecure.

3. Our insecure feelings are increased as we move through childhood. This takes place when a child expresses normal feelings, such as anger or even sadness. Some of these normal expressions of feelings are not tolerated in many homes. For example, how many of you could openly

express anger toward your parents and not be reprimanded? When we were sad how often did parents tell us not to cry? When parents try to cheer up a sad child, a message is communicated to the child that his/her feelings are not accepted. Children are left with a subconscious fear that our natural self, who has feelings, is not lovable and somehow feelings are wrong or bad. We learn to guard and even suppress our feelings. This adds to our insecurity.

Many of the things parents say to children are not intended to promote insecure feelings. Take a close look at some of the verbal and non-verbal messages children receive and assess how they can leave children feeling.

You are: not good enough; too loud; too quiet; selfish; stupid; opinionated; lazy; irresponsible; never satisfied; just like your father/mother/brother/ sister; too fat/skinny.
You always . . .
You can't do anything right; you don't deserve . . .
You should have known better.
You never try hard enough.
You disappointed me (translated: you are a disappointment).
Why don't you stop being so . . .

Take a moment and add to this list. What messages did you receive that contributed to your insecure feelings? This is not intended to blame parents. Blaming others is a waste of time and energy. Besides, our parents were doing the best job they knew how. But you can stop that cycle.

4. There are various stages in life where we feel powerless and out-of-control. Children often feel as if they have little control over what is happening in their lives. Parents, the big people in their lives, control their daily activities. Witness the behavior of children when they are not in control. Crying and temper tantrums are the norm. When a young child does not have control and is literally dependent upon the parent for his/her physical and emotional needs, feelings of helplessness naturally follow, and thus insecurity. Children begin to feel that the way to have a sense of control over their lives is to influence their parent's response. They figure out that a positive response from

parents comes by doing <u>and</u> feeling what is expected. This compliancy is accompanied by the insecurity of not being in control.

Then, typically, parents add to the insecurity of a child by the use of fear or guilt to get a child to behave. Controlling a child's behavior with threats and/or guilt may get the desired results. The fear and guilt, also, contribute to a child's feeling of insecurity.

My parents used guilt, fear, anger and love to get me to do what they expected. I think I turned out fairly normal and have the usual degree of insecure and secure feelings.

The control issues that surround a marriage also lead to insecurity. The power and control issues in a marriage include: sex, fighting, competition, gender roles and money.

Money is power. We feel powerful, independent and self-reliant when we have money. We feel helpless, dependent and insecure when money is scarce or our spouse is making decisions about money that do not make sense to us. Couples are unlikely to deal effectively and creatively with issues of money until they acknowledge and discuss how their need to be in control affects money matters.

Whether the subject is money or something else, couples may not even remember what they were fighting about after a few days have passed. The reason: most fights are not about a particular issue so much as about giving in, i.e. power and control.

Power and control are reflected in these words that are often heard when referring to a marriage: "Henpecked," "Head of the household," "Wrapped around his/her finger," "That's my thing," "Who wears the pants in the family?"

The accepted and expected roles males and females carry into a marriage relates to the issue of power and control. The change in traditional roles and expectations for males and females has added to feelings of insecurity.

For centuries, men have been the dominant gender or, at least, thought they were and acted as if they were. Women have come to understand it is not healthy in male/female relationships for men to think and demonstrate they have more power and control. When a male is viewed as insecure it is deemed unmanly. A woman's insecurities communicate she is weak and submissive. Men add to feelings of insecurity by living all their lives trying to show control and power, even when they feel weak and vulnerable. In an effort to avoid the stereotype of being weak and helpless, a woman may overreact as a way to retain and display power and control. Couples often get into this cycle and have no idea how to stop it.

Power and control are also played out in how men and women handle expectations at home and at work. Everyone desires some authority, at least, in some area. For example, a husband who works outside the home has a degree of control in his work. He feels insecure when he walks into the house and realizes his authority is not absolute. The wife who works inside the home also has a degree of control over her work. All day she has control over the house and children. Her husband walks into the house and continues his pattern of being in control. She feels her power and control are compromised. Both end up feeling insecure about themselves and their roles.

We have little control over what is happening around us or at least, we feel we have little control. We feel insecure when we see what is or is not happening in our lives and world. War, poverty, disease, economy, weather and injustice are a few of the issues that leave us feeling insecure because we cannot control these life experiences.

5. Our insecurities are connected to external appearance. We have let our society fill us with messages about the importance of physical attributes. In subtle and not so subtle ways, we have allowed others to define what the ideal body should look like.

These feelings of insecurity are especially relevant when it comes to the sexual parts of our bodies. Feelings of insecurity stem from how we do or do not measure up to society's definition of what is sexy. For example, we often think certain body parts need to be well proportioned, the "right" size, not too little and not too large. We allow body fat to define how attractive we view ourselves or our spouse. We tend to think that our bodies are a turnoff to our spouse because of how society defines a sexy body.

As we get older and some part or parts of our body are not attractive and proportioned as we want, we do not feel sexy and appealing. The feelings get in the way of receiving our spouse's sexual advances as well as initiating lovemaking.

Addressing our insecure feelings comes with positive self-esteem, resulting from confidence that our inner beauty is more important than our external appearance.

6. How do you feel when someone criticizes you or puts you down?

As I reflect on my years as a pastor, I recall how I did and did not deal with criticism. At the conclusion of a worship service six hundred people could shake my hand and compliment me on my sermon. But if one person was critical, I would spend most of Sunday afternoon being obsessed with that one comment. Why would I continue to be upset about one negative comment? Criticism brings out the magnitude of our insecurities.

Being criticized by others will always be part of our life experience. Someone may be critical of something you said or did. Or you may have accomplished or achieved something, and someone tells you it was unimportant. We have feelings of insecurity when someone treats us unfairly.

Check out your feelings of insecurity (defensiveness) when your spouse says: "Why don't you . . ." "You always do/say . . ." "I can't understand why you . . ." "You never . . ." "When will you ever . . ." "When you do/ say that you are so . . ." "It seems to me you should . . ." "When are you going to realize . . ." You can fill in the dots and take notice of your feelings of insecurity.

Although you are not responsible for your spouse's feelings of insecurity, your relationship will be enhanced when you decide to eliminate the following words from your vocabulary: you should; you ought; you need to; you must; you cannot. These words are usually received as criticism and fan the flame of your spouse's insecurities.

While many of our insecurities come from the criticism and disapproval of others, they also arise from *self* criticism. Failure, including the failure to accomplish a goal, is frequently accompanied by being disappointed in ourselves. Our disappointment may be tempered by knowing that, at least, we tried. A lot of good things happen—even in the face of failure. Failure is a normal part of anyone who sets out to accomplish a goal. Therefore, in the presence of failure, a degree of insecurity is normal to all who strive to achieve.

7. Feelings of insecurity often come from rejection. All of us have had the experience of being rejected. The rejection may feel unjustified and unfair. Because of our experiences of rejection, we carry those insecure feelings into every relationship, anticipating the rejection may come sooner or later.

My first memory of being rejected was in the first grade. My first girl friend let me know she liked another boy better than me. Like you, I could add numerous other examples of rejection that continue to live within our psyche.

All of us feel secure when we are loved and accepted. We feel secure when others think we are important and valued. The problem arises from the fact that most of the time the love that comes to us is conditional. We are valued and considered important *if* we are nice, good, responsible and hard working. We experience this as rejection. This experience of conditional love and the normal response of feeling insecure are present in every relationship.

If you put your hand on a stove and it is hot, the next time you will be reluctant to touch the stove. Will or will you not get burned? The same holds true in our relationship with others. Once we have been burned/rejected, we feel insecure. We can expect to have those insecure feelings of uncertainty, inadequacy, suspicion and distrust.

In many relationships we do not get burned/rejected. Nevertheless, our insecurities are always present in some degree. The degree depends, of course, on the frequency and intensity of rejection and also on how we choose to respond to being burned.

8. Our insecurities are being triggered by the way our society determines what and who is of value. "What did you get in biology?" Does our grading system contribute to our insecurities as we are compared to others who get "better" grades? What value is placed on where a person lives, the size of his/her house, car or bank account? If you or your team "beat" the other person/team, how are you looked upon? Athletic events and competition can be enjoyable. They can even teach us lessons about life. But our insecurities are revealed when sports can influence whether we feel good about ourselves. Why are crowds at sporting events much lower when the team is losing?

9. Who among us would not feel insecure in the face of our own mortality? We or someone we love could die in the next minute, next month, day or year. Life is full of death experiences such as divorce, a move, a change in life's circumstance or deteriorating health.

Some people try to avoid their feelings of insecurity in the face of their own death. They deal with their insecurity by immersing themselves in work, drugs, entertainment or religion. Authentic religion is not meant to be a way of avoiding the realities and problems of everyday life by clinging to hope of heaven. Rather faith gives us power to live a life of love and service to others in the midst of our insecurities.

10. Because we are so insecure, do we need to focus on changing? Change itself brings insecurity. Change is accompanied by the unknown. Change implies something is going to be different. Sameness carries with it a certain amount of security. The unknown and uncertainty that accompany change raise our level of anxiety and insecurity. If we change, what will the outcome look like? We have no assurance the change will make things better.

When life circumstances are going as we want and problems seem non-existent or distant, it is fairly easy to convince ourselves that we are more secure than insecure. But we know how quickly life circumstances can change.

I'm sure you may have other security-robbing life experiences to add to the list, but the ten I have listed are some of the most common.

Many people deny they have insecure feelings. They smugly proclaim they do not allow themselves to be negatively affected by the circumstances of life. In fact, some of the most insecure people I have met have been those who go out of their way to project self-confidence. Deciding how we are going to respond to the circumstances of life is to be valued. Yet, it is my experience that we tend to camouflage our insecurities by appearing to be self-assured and confident.

At our marriage seminars, we ask couples to examine the degree to which they and their spouse are secure and insecure. In the past, Elaine has tended to see me as being more secure than insecure, even though I have told her I feel more insecure than secure. Why does she see me differently than I see myself? Does she have a need to see me as being more secure than insecure? Do I have a need for her to see me as being secure? Do I mask my insecurities even with her?

When it comes to the degree of each other's secure and insecure feelings, communicating your ideas are more important than whether you agree on how you perceive each other. Share your reluctance to tell yourself or your spouse that feelings of insecurity outweigh secure feeling. Recognizing one's insecurities is a sign of strength, not weakness. Insecurity is only a sign of weakness in a marriage when one or both partners fail to recognize their insecurities and share them with each other.

Some people think nothing good can come from focusing on the negative. Insecure feelings are not negative. They are simply feelings. It is not negative for couples to deal with reality. Dealing positively with marriage problems and issues comes as a result of facing squarely what some define as negative feeling.

I hope you have a strong sense of inner security and self-love. Also, I hope it has become clearer that you have a greater degree of insecure feelings than secure feelings. I trust this information will be received as positive rather than negative.

Why have I devoted so many paragraphs pointing out how our life experiences lead to insecure feelings? Why emphasize that we are more insecure than secure? There are five reasons why identifying, claiming, examining and understanding our insecurities are important to a healthy marriage.

1. There is an elephant in the house of marriage

If there was an elephant in your house, can you imagine the consequences if you decided to ignore it? While the elephant presents some problems, the problems will get worse, unless you decide to deal with the elephant head on. We may wish the elephant wasn't in the house, but wishing doesn't make the elephant disappear. There are a number of other things happening in the house beside the elephant. But it makes sense to make the presence of the elephant a priority. All of the "other things" in the house will be greatly affected by the elephant.

Our insecurities are the biggest elephant in a marriage. Just imagine the consequences of ignoring each spouse's insecurities. While our insecurities present problems for the relationship, the problems will get worse unless we decide to deal with them head on. We may wish there were not so many insecure feelings surrounding our relationship, but wishing doesn't make the insecurities disappear. There are many issues happening in the marriage; but it makes sense to make the presence of our insecurities a priority. Everything else in the marriage is affected by this elephant, our insecurities.

2. Self-awareness begins with acknowledging our insecurities

Growing a strong marriage is tied closely to each partner having healthy self-awareness.

My wife and I were discussing this issue. She said to me, "If people are so insecure, is there any hope that marriages can be good?" My response was, "Yes, if couples are aware of their insecurities."

Claiming our insecurities is power for dealing with them in a healthy manner. A sense of personal power, in the midst of our insecurities, is one of the best gifts we can give our spouse. Being self-aware of our insecurities enables us to enter the process of developing and increasing our self-esteem, self-love.

3.   Keeping our focus

Examining our insecurities has to do with keeping the focus where it is most productive and healthy. All too often, when problems arise in the marriage we tend to focus on our spouse's issues and insecurities rather than upon our own. Getting each spouse to focus on their own feelings of insecurity is one of the biggest challenges I have faced in marriage counseling. Inevitably couples will come into my office and begin talking about what their spouse is or is not doing. There is resistance when I invite them to focus upon their own feelings of insecurity and not those of their spouse.

Dealing with our own insecurities is all we can handle. Positive things happen when we focus on our own insecurities. Attention to our own insecurities minimizes blaming our spouse.

4.   Dealing with conflict in a healthy way

Conflict originates in our insecurities. Out of our insecurities comes the need to win and be right. We are eager to let our spouse know our way of dealing with a certain situation is not only different but better. Out of our insecurities we have a need to inform our spouse that we have more knowledge than they have about any number of topics. We are eager to let our spouse know the way a certain situation was handled is not the way we would have handled it. We become defensive when our spouse points out we made a mistake or we are wrong. This can be traced to our insecurities.

5.   Acknowledging our insecurities helps avoid depending on our spouse to bolster our self-worth and value.

Too often, relationships are strained and even broken as a result of one or both individuals depending upon the other for their happiness. The relationship is driven by neediness, rather than by a person's individual self-esteem, strength and self-love.

Depending upon our partner for our happiness leaves the partner with a mandate to do for us what ultimately we can only do for ourselves. Feelings of pressure are the consequence that comes with being asked to take responsibility for our partner's happiness. Rather than being self-reliant and standing on our own two feet, we are depending upon our lover to hold us up. Asking someone to hold us up, in time, gets heavy. There is a big difference in a relationship when we take responsibility for our own feelings and actions, rather than being dependent upon our spouse.

Being dependent upon our spouse to fulfill our needs leaves us taking and getting from each other rather than giving. Yes, giving to our spouse without regard for what we might receive is a dimension of love. But the relationship gets distorted when we depend upon our spouse to such a degree that we discount or ignore our own needs. Putting our spouse's needs before our own can enhance love, unless it is at the price of denying our own needs. All too often our insecurities keep us from a healthy balance of declaring our own wants and, at the same time, giving the needed attention to our spouse's needs.

This morning I was listening to songs on my ipod. I noticed how many of the love songs communicate that love is being dependent upon someone else for our happiness. I heard words such as, "I can't live without you," "Without you there is no day," "I am no good without you," "Without you I am nothing," and "I won't be happy until you are happy." I am sure you can add to the list.

I recall the words from a popular movie where the man said to his lover, "You complete me." We all need and want love. Indeed having another's love is helpful to our feeling secure. Being dependent upon our spouse to feel complete is unhealthy to growing marital love.

Does this mean when we have a high degree of self-love there isn't a need for another's love, i.e. we do not need to be married to be happy and fulfilled?

Happiness and fulfillment in a marriage come primarily from each spouse standing strong on his/her own sense of self-worth and self-love. Such persons do not need another's love to feel good about themselves. Our own song of love is good and beautiful. A marriage makes the song sound even better.

Some years ago, a popular love song said, "You light up my life." Needing, wanting, expecting and depending upon another to bring love's light into our lives is a set-up for an unhealthy relationship. Healthy marriages happen when each individual recognizes he/she has lots of love within. Two people come together to share their light. This is important when life's path has become dark. With marriage the light becomes stronger and brighter. The shared light has a lasting and power-filled quality that is helpful in this world of turmoil.

Because every person has a good amount of insecurity, it is inevitable that there will be times when each of us depends, to some degree, upon another for our sense of worth and value. To say dependency is unhealthy and we need to be secure within ourselves is easier said than done. In fact, without people around us who support and encourage us, we find ourselves imprisoned in our insecure feelings. It is, therefore, imperative that we do what is necessary to have a strong sense of self-worth and at the same time draw upon the love and affirmation of others.

Scott Peck in his book, *The Road Less Traveled*, addresses this point: "Ultimately all couples learn that true acceptance of their own and each other's individuality and separateness is the only foundation upon which a true marriage can be based and real love can grow." (p. 93)

The Bible speaks of "two becoming one." "God made them male and female. For this reason a man shall leave his father and mother and be joined to his wife, and the two shall become one. So they are no longer two but one." (Mark 10:7-8) In one sense this is truth and to be valued. In another sense, this truth must not override the importance of remaining strong and secure within oneself. Two self-confident, independent, secure and self-loving people come together and become one. In becoming one, each is careful to remain strong and confident within his or her own being.

With all of our insecurities, it is a miracle there are any healthy marriages. Just because all of us are more insecure than secure, does this mean we should not get married or all is hopeless?

The large amount of insecure feelings that we possess need not be viewed as a prescription for pessimism or despair. The degree of insecurity in each spouse can be turned into something positive. Good things happen when our insecure feelings are identified, owned and shared. Hope and change come not by berating ourselves for having insecure feelings. Rather hope and change come through accepting the truth that beneath our insecurities is a competent and love-filled person.

Hope also resides in communicating with our spouse about our insecurities. The best gift you can give your partner is to become knowledgeable about the nature of your insecurities and then share your awareness with your spouse. Even if you disagree with my premise that we are more insecure than secure, discussing it will open up issues important to a healthy marriage. The vulnerability that comes through sharing insecure feelings increases closeness.

Some years ago, Elaine and I were doing our morning jog. Elaine would always run farther and faster. On this morning she was falling behind me. She even stopped several times while I jogged on, patting myself on the back that I was in better shape. This happened for several days before I confronted her. She thought the tiredness was caused by a terrible cold she had several weeks prior. After another week of the same pattern, I demanded that she see a doctor. She was diagnosed with chronic leukemia. Over the next months she received medical treatment. In time, she was declared in remission. The medical people use the word "remission" not "cured". Disaster would have followed if she had continued to ignore what was happening in her body. Things changed significantly when she acknowledged what was happening, understood the nature of the illness and entered into a process that brought health.

It is not inevitable that our insecurities lead to an unhealthy marriage. If we ignore them, we can predict disaster will follow. Our insecurities cannot be cured. They are a normal part of each of us. Things will change significantly in a marriage when we acknowledge our insecurities, understand the nature of the insecurities and enter into a process that brings health to our married love. And maybe our insecurities will lessen in intensity and degree.

As I was making my final read of this chapter, Elaine and I had three days of tension in our relationship. We both said things that resulted in hurt and anger. It took me the full three days to realize the source of the problem was the fact that my insecurities were working overtime. The next time there is tension and problems in your marriage, I would suggest you beat my record of three days. See if you can, in a shorter amount of time, recognize the source of your marital tension is found in your insecure feelings working overtime.

It is one thing to identify our insecurities and acknowledge that they affect the marriage relationship. It is quite another thing, and far more important, to identify _how_ we can turn the insecurities into a positive resource for growing a healthy marriage. This includes becoming less insecure. It is fairly easy to identify our insecure feelings, but it can be a major challenge to come up with answers on how to deal effectively with those insecurities and become more secure. For insights on how we can turn our insecurities into a positive force, I invite you to deliberate on the content of the next chapter.

At one of our marriage workshops, after the session on being insecure, a man raised his hand and asked, "OK, you've convinced me that I am more insecure than secure. But what can I do to become more secure? Is there something more I can do besides being aware of my insecurities and examining the sources?"

I suggested he eat the right kind of food. He looked at me with shock and said, "What do you mean? What is the right kind of food that would make me less insecure?" I told him to make certain that he consumed as much grace (unconditional love) as possible, especially God's Grace.

God's Grace is a free gift. You can read more about this free gift in the Bible, Romans 5:12-20. You can make this Grace an integral part of your life by touching and being touched by the message and ministry of Jesus Christ. He gives the food that does not perish, but lasts (John 6:27).

And hopefully you have some people in your life who, at times, will feed you grace as they love you unconditionally. Focusing on loving your spouse unconditionally is the way to ensure that grace abounds.

Your self-esteem will improve dramatically as you accept the truth that your value and worth are not dependent upon anything you do or don't do. Neither is it dependent upon what others think. This is the nature and wonder of God's Grace. Receive this Grace and you will become more secure.

I want to offer this final word of caution before you and your spouse discuss this chapter, using the questions below. Arguments can easily occur when talking about our insecurities, especially when we talk about our spouse's insecurities. Therefore, after you complete Question #1 below, do the following: First, rather than being upset with your spouse when she/he indicates you are more insecure than secure, be upset with me. I am the one who believes everyone has a greater degree of insecure feelings than secure. Second, together examine the reasons listed in this chapter as to why everyone has a large amount of insecure feelings. Third, spend much more time talking about your own insecurities, rather than your spouse's.

QUESTIONS FOR PERSONAL RELECTION
AND
DISCUSSION WITH YOUR SPOUSE

KISS 1: How do you see yourself—secure or insecure? We are all a little of both, so put a percentage to it, e.g. "I am 60 percent secure and 40 percent insecure or 65 percent insecure and 35 percent secure or . . ." Do the same exercise/percentage for how you view your spouse. Discuss your answers.

KISS 2: Do you agree or disagree with the premise that you and your spouse have a greater degree of insecure than secure feelings? Why? Why not? Are you reluctant to acknowledge your insecurities? Why? Why not?

KISS 3: How do the control issues listed above impact upon your marriage?

KISS 4: What life experiences contribute to your feelings of insecurity? How are they noticeable in your marriage?

KISS 5: Discuss the way you are or are not dependent upon your spouse for your happiness and self-esteem?

KISS 6: Discuss how your individual insecurities shape your relationship. Share why you agree or disagree that the presence of insecurity is not a reason for alarm.

3

Receive and Activate Your Power

Ava Lou came to me for marriage counseling—alone. She started the session by bemoaning the fact that her husband would not come with her and quickly jumped to the subject of her husband's many faults. I let her go on for a minute but then stopped her unproductive tirade.

I said to her, "I really don't think it is a wise use of our time to focus on your husband since he isn't here. Why don't you tell me how you are contributing to the marital difficulties?" I could tell by her face that she was resisting my encouraging her to examine her own insecurities.

By our fourth session, Ava Lou walked in and said, "OK, so I have insecurities. Tell me how to get rid of them." I reminded her that the elephant is not going away. We don't get rid of our insecurities. We learn how to deal with them.

Increasing self-esteem and self-love is the most productive way to deal with our insecurities and, therefore, our relational problems.

Simply being aware of our insecurities is not enough. We must learn how to activate the power that is needed for increasing love of self.

Let's ask ourselves this question: Given the nature of my insecurities, how can I begin dealing with them in a healthy manner and thereby enhance my marriage?

Here are six ways for receiving and activating your power, power that is needed for becoming more secure.

I. First, power comes through a *lifestyle* of comprehensive self- examination.

The word "lifestyle" is important. Understanding all that is involved in feelings of insecurity calls for consistent and continual self-examination of both our limitations and our strengths.

Such a lifestyle includes examining the numerous messages and experiences that contribute to our insecurity. Many of these messages and experiences occurred early in life and lie deep within us. Self-examination means naming and claiming the feelings that surround our insecurities. What situations and people trip our insecurity button?

Because a true self-examination exposes our limitations and frailties, many people choose not to do so. Many of us have troubling pasts, so why unnecessarily dig up uncomfortable issues? Letting the past remain the past isn't always a healthy choice. It has been my experience that the rewards of a life-style of self-examination far outweigh any discomfort.

God already knows what lies within each of us. God knows our past better than we do. God understands all that is involved in what has happened and why it has happened. God understands the emotions that surround the past. And certainly God forgives the past.

When we do decide to be honest with ourselves and let go of past incidents that may contribute to our insecurities, we activate power in our lives by believing God knows, understands and forgives.

Many of us have discovered we need assistance in doing an honest self-examination. I have difficulty being objective when it comes to recognizing and evaluating areas of my personality that need growth. Over the years, books, family members, friends, support groups, and individual and group therapy have greatly enhanced my times of self-examination.

Don't know where to start? Well, identifying our strengths is a good place to begin the process. Make sure your strengths are truly yours, and not ones that have been projected on to you by other people.

A physician named Lee came to see me one day. His father and grandfather were doctors; and as a youngster, many expected him to be a doctor. Because of this, he assumed medicine was his calling and strength. But once he had his own practice, he didn't feel the fulfillment that he thought he would. Through self-examination, he realized medicine was not his passion. He had let others influence him so greatly that he never even took time to examine his own dreams. Fulfillment came when he chose a different profession.

Carefully and prayerfully assess your abilities. Dare to dream. Don't allow yourself to be stymied by how others define success.

II. Power comes by recognizing, claiming and activating your personal power.

A. Where is your focus?

Oftentimes I have thought our marriage would improve if only my wife would change certain things she says and does. I focused on my wife's actions and attitudes rather than my own. However, I now realize, when I do this, I am giving away my power.

I recall the first time this truth became very clear. Several years ago, Elaine and I decided to seek counseling as the way of dealing with a problem that was continually causing tension in our marriage: being punctual.

I began the session by telling the counselor about how Elaine is always late. "Always?" said the counselor. "Well, maybe not always, but far too often to suit me. "The counselor responded to me, "You have a problem." Looking at Elaine I said, "You bet I do." Finally someone understood. But

33

the counselor quickly knocked me off of my pedestal when he said, "Let me restate what I said. You are the problem."

I quickly came to my defense, "What do you mean I am the problem? She is the one who is late. She is inconsiderate of my feelings and the feelings of others who have to wait on her."

"Why don't you get a divorce?" said the counselor. I didn't want a divorce. That was ridiculous. I just wanted her to change and be more sensitive to being on time. Is that expecting too much?

The counselor continued, "If you don't want to get a divorce I see only two options left for you. You can wait until she changes and continue the anger and hurt, or you can change your response when she is late." Because this pattern had been going on for many years, I was smart enough to realize she was not going to change.

Then a light bulb came on: when I saw Elaine as the problem, I was failing to claim and use my power. I was acting like a victim.

I could not control what Elaine decided to do. I could only control my response. I needed all of the personal power I could generate in order to respond in a more intelligent manner. By claiming my power, I was ready for the counselor to help me understand how and why I was responding so angrily to her lateness.

Elaine continues to be late. However, two things have happened as a result of claiming my power. First, she's not late nearly as often as she used to be. When I quit pouring guilt and anger on Elaine, she got more punctual on her own. Secondly, when she is late, rather than getting mad, I focus on using my power to respond differently. This power enables me to figure out ways of responding that make sense as an adult rather than responding like a little child.

We give our power away when we waste time and energy focusing on our spouse's insecurities rather than examining our own. If you think your spouse is the cause of marital tension, then you must wait until she/he changes before the situation gets any better. Your power is given away to your spouse.

B.   Watch Your Words

While dealing with this issue, I also learned that not only how we speak affects our power, but so does what we say. Our personal power is compromised when we use certain words, such as "can't," "try" and "make me feel."

There are some things we literally *can't* do. For example, I can't dunk a basketball or hit a golf ball 400 yards. But most of the time "can't" is used when we actually could, but decide that we either don't want to do something and/or feel helpless. Using the word, *can't*, gives away our power.

A woman named Mary once told me about one of her husband's personality traits that drove her crazy. After going on and on about it, she said to me, "I can't live like this."

I asked her to change the word "can't" to "decide" and say out loud, "I've decided not to live like this." At first, she resisted. But a light went on when she said the sentence and replaced "can't" with "decide." She realized the word *can't* was giving her power to her husband. Using the word *decide* enabled her to understand she had the power to decide what she would or would not do in this difficult situation.

Mary was going to need all the power she could muster in order to deal constructively with her husband's insecurities, as well as her own. Changing how she would respond to her husband was not going to be easy, but retaining her power made change possible. Refraining from using "can't" empowered her to recognize her options.

Another person who came to counseling for this issue was Ronald. He said to me, "I *can't* help it. I get so mad. My wife tries to run my life." I invited Ronald to claim his power by saying out loud, "When my wife runs my life I have *decided* to be mad." Changing the word "can't" to "decide" triggered his rational self and enabled him to see options other than getting mad.

Our power is also activated when we avoid using the word "try." *Trying* to do something is also consenting to give away our power.

For example, if I hold out a pencil and ask you to take it from me, what happens if you "try" to take it versus you actually take it. If you take it, you now have the pencil within your possession. If you *try* to take the pencil (versus actually taking it) you end up without a pencil in your hand.

Likewise, telling my wife I will try to be on time is very different than telling her I am "deciding" to be on time or "choosing" not to be on time.

Say out loud the following two sentences. "Honey, I will try to remember to pick up some toothpaste at the grocery store." "Honey, I will remember to pick up some toothpaste at the grocery store." Notice the difference in how each sentence feels to you and to your spouse. (Note: Be sure to say the sentence out loud.) When your spouse does or says something that has potential to create tension and conflict, "try" (oops) to keep your power. No. Don't try. Either keep your power or don't keep it. It's your decision. Using "try" gives away your power.

I suggested to a man that he should give his wife more compliments. He responded with, "I know that is a good idea and will try to do it." I replied, "Are you going to *try* to do it or are you going to *decide* to do it?"

Our power is also stolen when we tell our spouse how he/she makes us feel. We will say to our spouse, "You make me feel so mad" or "That makes me feel like you don't care." No one can make us feel something. Feelings belong to us and are not caused by our spouse. We choose to feel whatever it is we are feeling. We fail to take responsibility for ourselves and give away our power when we use the words, "make feel."

Some may dispute this idea by noting that when someone hurts us, physically or emotionally, feeling pain is inevitable. Someone may be able to physically make us feel pain, e.g. if they would hit us over the head with a bat. However, no one can *make* us feel emotional pain. To say someone is making us feel a certain feeling gives away our power. Blame, accusations and conflict are sure to follow.

I shared this illustration in my previous book, *Believe the Believable*. Turner, a young black man, went to see his pastor. "Pastor, I continually have to deal with racial slurs. You would think in this 21st century we would have moved beyond this kind of thing. It *makes* me so mad. I find myself getting angrier and angrier. I don't know what to do." The pastor responded to the young man: "Why are you *deciding* to be mad and listening to them? They are not talking to you. That is not who you are."

How are you going to respond to your spouse when he/she says things that are hurtful and trip your insecure feelings? A key to activating our inner power comes by replacing our "make feels" with an acknowledgment that we decide and choose what we feel.

C. What do you want?

Another important way to activate your power is by being clear with your spouse about what you *want*. Are you hesitant to let your spouse know what you want? This point is stressed in one of the better marriage books I have read, *Getting The Love You Want*, by Harville Hendrix.

Some will contend that asking for what you want is selfish and thus detrimental to the relationship. Asking for what you want can be selfish and detrimental when it is conditional, i.e. you are going to be disappointed *if* you don't get what you want.

Even if asking for what you want comes out of the selfish part of us, it is better than depending upon our spouse to read our mind. Most of us flunked mind reading in school. If what you want is important to your emotional health and to the marriage, then claim your power and let your spouse know what you want.

For a variety of reasons, our partner may not give us what we want. If we think the reason is invalid, we may decide to feel rejected and stop letting our spouse know what we want. This diminishes our power.

There is a difference between asking our spouse to fulfill our needs and asking for what we want. Asking our spouse to fulfill our needs falls into the trap of co-dependency. Our spouse is not responsible for satisfying our needs.

Asking our spouse to take care of us sets up a parent/child relationship, but telling our spouse what you want (not need) is an adult to adult transaction. "I want" is clear, assertive and non-gaming communication.

It is important to note that when asking for what you want, be as specific as possible. For example, it is one thing to tell your spouse you want to be appreciated. It is another thing to say you feel appreciated when they do or say . . . Consider saying, "I experience your love when you do/say . . ."

Letting your spouse know what you want is vital to healthy lovemaking. All too often we depend upon our spouse, indeed we expect our spouse, to give us satisfaction. This assumes he or she knows what satisfies us.

Of course, persons with low self-esteem feel they do not deserve to get what they want, let alone be confident enough to ask. Because of our insecurities we may not even let ourselves know what satisfies us, let alone tell our spouse. A woman may not ask for what she wants because she has not made the distinction between being assertive and being aggressive. A man may not be clear about what he wants because of being perceived as weak.

My wife had just listened to a sermon on the internet. The preacher suggested that a marriage is enriched when we say to our spouse, "How can I enhance your day/life?" Elaine wanted me to ask her this question. I said to her, "Why don't you just tell me what you want. What is so important about me asking?" She responded, "I don't know what it is. It's like you are giving me a gift and I don't have to ask. It frees me up. If I tell you what I want and you give it to me, it doesn't mean as much as when you ask me what I want. This is especially true when you see that I am having a stressful day. When you say, 'How can I enhance your day?,' it feels like you are reaching out to me."

Elaine and I continued our conversation about letting each other know what we want versus asking our spouse what he/she wants. We concluded both are important. If your spouse is stressed, it may be more important to take the initiative and ask what he/she wants.

Letting our spouse know what we want does not always produce the results we want. I recall several years ago when Elaine and I were having tension about the various responsibilities around the house. We made a list and negotiated who would do what. She wanted me to help with the laundry. She said she would take the dirty clothes to the laundry room, put in the soap and begin the process. I was to take the clothes out of the washer, put them in the dryer and transfer them to the bedroom. I did what she wanted. An argument started when I did not do it the way she wanted. I felt like I had two options: I could tell her if she didn't like the way I did it she could do it herself or I could do it the way she would do it. Neither option seemed viable to me. Could a compromise be met?

Telling your spouse what you want can turn into an argument, depending upon several factors.

First, *how* it is said is important. For example, the other night Elaine expressed a "want" in regards to our kitchen. She said, "I want you to put your dirty dishes into the dishwasher and stop leaving them in the sink." What if she had said, "I like when dirty dishes are put in the dishwasher and not left in the sink? Would you be willing to do that for me?"

When we tell our spouse what we want is an important second factor. A few minutes before the comment about the sink, she had criticized me for doing something. Therefore, when she told me what she wanted I felt she was being critical of me, again. In that moment, I saw her as my mother and responded like a belligerent little boy. She responded in like fashion and World War III began.

What if Elaine had expressed her "want" at another time? For example, on our date night when we were at a restaurant what if she had said, "Honey, keeping the kitchen as clean as possible is important to me. I would like for both of us to be more intentional about putting dirty dishes into the dishwasher after we are done eating." Also, if she said this same sentence late at night when I was tired, she might get a different response than if she said it early in the morning.

Some may feel badly if they actually get what they want.

For years, Beatrice's husband came home from work, ate supper and relaxed in front of the TV while she cooked the meal, did the dishes, finished the laundry and prepared the two preschool children for bed. All of this was after she had spent a full day looking after the kids and house. After Barry had read the newspaper, enjoyed his favorite TV program and his wife had put the kids to bed, he approached her about having sex. You can probably guess how she responded. And you can also guess how Barry reacted to his wife's refusal.

After receiving some counseling, she gave herself permission to ask for what she wanted. She asked Barry to read the bedtime stories to the children, give them baths and put them to bed. After several nights, Beatrice admitted she felt uncomfortable. She had difficulty giving up control over what she felt was her responsibility. She felt guilty when she got what she asked. This is where continual self-examination is helpful. Learn to understand why you might feel guilty about receiving what you asked for.

D. Give Back

Another way that our personal power is activated is when we give back. Increasing your love of self comes by doing love, focusing our love and gifts on helping others.

This is a fact of life: God designed our lives in such a way that we feel better when we give love away. Emotional and sometimes even physical sickness is the result of not giving our love. Keeping love for ourselves betrays the purpose of God's gift. We activate our power through sharing our love and, therefore, living life as God intended.

Jesus said it this way: "For whoever would save his life will lose it, and whoever loses her life for my sake will find it." (Matthew 16:25) We find power for living and loving when we decide to move beyond being pre-occupied with our own needs and give ourselves to the needs of others. Acts of compassion and generosity lead many to renewed power. This power enables us to improve our self-image.

Indeed there are lots of people who are hungry, hungry for love and food. The need for us to offer our gifts is enormous.

A pastor of an inner-city church worked with a woman who was poor and had low self-esteem. He was having little success communicating to her the love of God so she could love herself. One day he asked her to help teach a children's Sunday school class. She told him that she did not know anything about the Bible or God. The pastor sensed she had a lot of love within her. After she had assisted in the class for several months, one of the little children said to her, "Are you related to Jesus?" Through the act of loving in the Sunday school class she began to understand and experience God's love. And, of course, her love of herself began to emerge. Her self-esteem improved. She had a new sense of inner strength.

I offer this word of caution: A person's motivation for helping others is important. I have known couples who decided to volunteer for a worthwhile cause. Their purpose was to help their troubled marriage. Helping others was their way of avoiding the issues that were causing tension in the marriage. With time, helping others lost its power.

E. God's Power

Depending upon our own power can accomplish many great things. I also know that much more can be accomplished by depending upon God's power.

I believe in the value of self-examination. I realize how I give away my power. I am keenly aware of the importance of giving back. But, all too often I find myself not doing what I know is best, for me, others and God. The words from the seventh chapter of Paul's letter to the Romans hit home to me: "For I do not do what I want, but I do the very thing I hate . . . I can will what is right but I don't do it. For I do not do the good I want, but the evil I do not want is what I do." We do need the power of God.

41

God's power is at work within each person. The Bible reminds us that each person is made in God's image. There is within each person a spark of divine power, waiting to be activated and grown. An effective way of dealing with our insecurities comes through trusting this seed of God's power, given to us at birth. Jesus said it this way, "The kingdom of God is within you." (Luke 17:2l) Another translation of this verse says, "God is inside us."

People have experienced the power of God in many different ways. The power has come to some through the miracles and mystery of nature. For others the experience of God's power has come through the birth of a baby. Art and music are also ways that we connect to God's power.

Power that endures is found in God's grace, i.e. unconditional love. This power of God is contrasted with the kind of power that is disseminated throughout our culture. In our society, value, worth and esteem are determined by how we perform, the degree of success we achieve and our good deeds.

Experiencing Christ's presence in my life has been the best way I have found for connecting to God's unconditional love.

Self-centeredness will negatively affect our performance goals. Personal limitations will impact our desire to be successful. Sin will subvert our striving to be a good person. Because we do not always live up to what others expect of us or what we expect of ourselves, fear and guilt emerge. Fear and guilt may produce many positive results. Fear, guilt and conditional love weaken our power and sabotage any positive results.

God's Grace is filled with power that frees us from the bondage of guilt and fear. The power of God's Grace comes to us as a free gift. We cannot earn it. We do not deserve it. We do not have to prove ourselves in order to be of worth and value to God. The only response to such a gift, at least the only response that makes sense, is gratitude. Faith is another word for gratitude. Grateful and faith-filled people experience the power needed for enhancing self-esteem and doing what is necessary for making love strong.

F.   Prayer's Power

I recall a time in my life when I was disillusioned with prayer. I now realize it was because my understanding of prayer was limited and incomplete.

Meaningful prayer returned to my life when I made two decisions. First, I freed myself from limiting my prayers to times when I had my eyes closed, began with Dear God, and concluded with Amen. Although this form of prayer has meaning to me, the most meaningful times of prayer are during my morning walk when my eyes are wide open and there is no beginning or ending.

Secondly, I begin approaching prayer as an opportunity to receive power rather than getting answers or informing God on what needed to happen in order for my life and the world to improve.

I used to believe when I came to a crossroads in my life and did not know which path to take, if I prayed God would reveal to me the right road/decision. I now believe that through prayer I receive God's power. It is this power that enables me to consider the options, make difficult decisions and not worry if my decision is right. As I look back on my life, many of my decisions involved relationships. The situation was too convoluted for me to stress about whether I had all the answers or even an answer that was absolutely correct. Prayer does not eliminate ambiguity and uncertainty. Prayer provides me the power I need to deal with ambiguity and uncertainty in a productive way.

Does God really answer our prayers? What did Jesus mean when he said we will get whatever we ask for in prayer? "Ask and it will be given to you . . ." (Luke 11:9) "Whatever you ask for in prayer, believe that you receive it, and you will." (Mark 11:23)

To understand these Scripture passages and answer the questions about how God answers prayer, examine closely the context of the passage.

In Mark's Gospel, the words about prayer follow the use of a metaphor. If someone tells a mountain to be cast into the sea and they believe, it will come to pass. (Mark 11:23) The Bible's use of metaphor is common.

There are problems in life that feel like obstacles as big as a mountain. Jesus does not mean if you pray to be healed, you will be healed. Prayer makes a significant difference when it comes to health issues. God's power helps us remove the mountains and obstacles that may be contributing to a particular health situation.

A teenage boy was struggling with how to resist feeling like a victim. He was born with a deformed leg. The leg was so shriveled and atrophied it could not bear much weight. As a small boy, he did not think much about it. However, as he grew older, he began to realize he could not do what the other kids were doing. He began to feel inferior. His parents noticed how he would brood over his limitations. His sense of powerlessness grew deeper and deeper. He became depressed and fearful. Then something happened that changed how he was responding to his situation.

One day his father confronted the son with what he was doing to himself. He told the boy about a big cathedral where there was a pile of braces and crutches left by people with disabilities like he had. These people had been healed. "I'm going to take you there," said the father. "We'll pray together and ask God to heal you so you can put your brace on that pile."

The boy was skeptical, yet he wanted to believe. The day arrived. The boy and his father entered the cathedral and went straight to the altar. The father told the boy to kneel. "Pray, son, and ask God to heal you." The boy decided he had nothing to lose. He would try anything. He was tired of feeling depressed, angry and scared. He prayed earnestly and began to hope maybe something good would happen. Out of the corner of his eye he noticed his father was crying. When the father saw the boy kneeling and praying, it bought tears to his eyes.

The boy stood up. He looked at his withered leg. It was the same as before. He began to walk down the aisle with his dad. He was limping as usual. The brace remained in place on his leg. As he approached the huge rear door of the church, something miraculous happened. He began to feel incredible warmth in his heart. He was not sure what had taken place. What he did realize was a sense of peace had overcome him. He said to his father, "Dad, you are right. I have been healed. God has not taken the brace off my leg. God has taken the brace off my mind." The brace on his leg remained in place. The boy had taken a crucial step toward being freed from his fears, depression and anger. Blame and self-pity were healed.

Prayer may or may not cure a physical illness or deformity. Prayer enables us to claim the power of God living within us. This power keeps us from succumbing to self-pity and blame. We are freed from feelings that get in our way of experiencing the fullness of life.

Does prayer work? Jesus says, whatever you ask for in prayer, believe and you will receive it. Believe what? Are we to believe that through prayer God can ensure a safe vacation trip, heal a disease, make us more secure than insecure or heal a broken marriage? These words of Jesus indicate a person already has what God gives through prayer. He says believe that you receive *it*. The *it* we receive is power already living within us. It waits to be activated through prayer. Does God answer prayer? No, God does not answer every question or solve every problem. Yes, through prayer God gives power whereby we are able to uncover answers to the complex and painful experiences of life and love. God does not do something *for* us. God empowers our minds and hearts so that we will accomplish great and creative things.

Surround each KISS with prayer. Don't look for easy answers. Do look for God's power to be activated through prayer. The power of prayer will enable you and your partner to sort out the many issues that surround a marriage, including dealing with our insecurities and enhancing self-esteem.

G. Surround Yourself with Loving People

For many of us, God's power has been activated through people who loved and accepted us even when we had thoughts and actions that were unlovable.

Part of what it means to believe and trust in God's power is to believe and trust there are people who understand the power of God's unconditional love and want to give that love to you. Surround yourself with people who accept your insecurities and readily offer you unconditional love.

Some years ago I received a phone call at two o'clock in the morning. I could not understand the person on the other end of the line. It was partially because I was half asleep and did not recognize the name. She said, "This is Mary Sue." She could tell by my silence that her name did not ring a bell. She continued, "Remember me? I was in your youth group." I began to realize who she was. While in college I served as youth director in a church adjacent to the campus. Mary Sue had been the president of our high school youth group at the church. I remembered her as a fine young woman. She was a leader and a devoted Christian. She had a positive influence on many of the youth of that church.

She asked if she could come to my house and talk with me. I said, "It is two o'clock in the morning. Is there a rush?" "Yes," she said. "I need to talk." I sensed urgency in her voice, so I told her to come.

I greeted her at the door. She had brought a friend with her. It had been more than five years since I had any contact with Mary Sue. She informed me she was a nurse in a local hospital. She also told me she had been drinking too much, as well as taking drugs. She reported a pattern of promiscuity. She began to cry as she told me her thoughts of killing herself. She was quick to tell me she no longer was involved in a church. She said, "My faith is gone. I'm not sure I believe in God anymore."

It was several years later that I again met with Mary Sue. I asked her how she was doing. She told me she was very involved in her church. Her job as a nurse had taken on new meaning. Her faith in God had returned and was stronger than ever. "What happened?" I inquired. "The last time we were together, you were very depressed. You told me you didn't believe in God anymore, and you were thinking about ending your life.

Mary Sue proceeded to tell me how the night in my living room changed her life. "Tell me about it. All I remember was saying things that, at the time, seemed irrelevant to what you were thinking and feeling. I knew you were feeling guilty. I remember trying to convince you that God forgave you. You simply shrugged off my words by reminding me that you no longer believed in God. I suggested you were too wrapped up in yourself and needed to get outside yourself and do something for others. You reminded me that you spent 40 hours a week working as a nurse. When you left that night, I felt as if I had been of no help at all. What helped turn your life around?"

Mary Sue responded. "Do you remember the last thing you did before I left?" I replied, "I guess I don't. It was over five years ago since you came to me." She continued, "You walked over to me. I was sitting on your couch. You did not say a word. You simply hugged my neck. I thought you would never let go. My friend joined in the group hug. It was the hug, more than all your words about God's forgiveness and unconditional love that restored my faith in God and myself. I knew you recognized my life was filled with sin and failure. Through your hug I felt God's power."

Mary Sue had low self-esteem. She was at least willing to make that phone call in order to surround herself with people she thought would extend unconditional love to her.

Power for improving your love of self and self-esteem will be enhanced by surrounding yourself with those who readily give unconditional love.

Many, certainly not all, of these people I have found in the church. I do not hear much about Grace during the week. The church is the one place that, on a regular basis, I hear and learn more about Jesus Christ. Find a church where each week you can experience the power of Jesus Christ. Through the life, teachings, crucifixion and resurrection of Christ, unconditional love can be experienced and serve as a dynamic source of power in your life.

I have received power through the love, support, life experiences and insights from a countless number of people—Elaine, family, counselors, friends, marriage seminars and support groups in the church. Chapter ten will expand on these experiences.

QUESTIONS FOR PERSONAL REFLECTION AND DISCUSSION WITH YOUR SPOUSE

KISS 1. How do you and your spouse feel about entering into a process of self- examination? Identify reasons why you may resist it.

KISS 2: List your strengths. List your spouse's strengths. Evaluate if the strength is what others expect of you or how to make the most money.

KISS 3: Use the words "can't" and "try" in a sentence. Now use the same sentence and replace it with "decide" or "choose." Notice the difference, including the power you feel, by replacing the words *can't* and *try* with *deciding* or *choosing*.

KISS 4: Say out loud a sentence that includes the words, "make feel." It would be helpful if it were a sentence you might say to your spouse. Change the words "make feel" to "I am deciding . . ." For example, "You make me so mad when you do that." "I am deciding to be mad at you when you do that." Share with your spouse your reactions to changing the wording.

KISS 5: On a scale of one to ten how proficient are you at letting your spouse know what you want? On the same scale, evaluate your spouse's proficiency. What is keeping you from being a ten?

KISS 6: What have been some experiences in your lifetime when *giving back* activated your power? Discuss some ways you would like to incorporate *giving back* into your marriage.

KISS 7: Talk about how your power is increased through the experience of Grace.

Discuss the understanding that faith is another word for gratitude. Share times when you have experienced the power of God's Grace as the result of being a recipient of unconditional love.

KISS 8: Share with each other your understanding of prayer. In what ways would you like to make prayer part of your marriage?

4

Why Do You Keep Doing And Saying Those Things?

Several years ago Elaine and I finally came to the point where we decided something had to be done about our repeated money feuds. Yes, we were just like the average American couple who fight about finances.

We realized the only way to stop hurting each other over this issue was to get counseling, but the counselor did not go about solving our problem the way we anticipated.

The counselor didn't waste her time, and, thankfully, our money, trying to resolve our differing views on money. Instead, the counselor asked us to do some self examination by revisiting our formative years and what we learned about money from our families of origin.

Understanding our psychological history pertaining to finances minimized our conflict. Understanding led to acceptance of our differences. While our ideas about money continue to be miles apart, the hurt has subsided through examining, understanding and accepting our psychological histories.

This is not only true when it comes to money, but in so many other areas. It can be freeing as a couple understands how our backgrounds influence our views.

Knowledge is power. We activate power for dealing with marital issues through knowledge of who we are and how we came to be that person. This includes understanding both the parts of our personality that are the result of genetic makeup and the parts that are the result of environmental factors. For example, is being outgoing or shy the result of genetics or environment?

Many of our feelings of insecurity lie within our subconscious and surface in unexpected and unhealthy ways. Examining our childhood brings to a conscious level the emotional baggage that often lives in our subconscious.

Many in the field of psychology believe our basic personalities are formed in the first two years of life. Some even suggest what takes place in the womb affects certain personality characteristics. Although there is no consensus on these views, all of us enter into marriage with entrenched patterns of thinking and feeling that have been programmed in us since childhood.

In his book, *Getting The Love You Want*, Harville Hendrix provides insight into this when he writes: "The feeling of unity that a child experiences in the womb and in the first few months of life gradually fades, giving way to a drive to be a distinct self. The essential state of unity remains, but there is a glimmer of awareness of the external world. It is during this stage of development that the child makes the monumental discovery that its mother is not always there . . . A child's success at feeling both distant from and connected to its mother has a profound impact on all later relationships. If the child is fortunate, he will be able to make clear distinctions between himself and other people but still feel connected to them. A child who has painful experiences early in life will either feel cut off from those around him or will attempt to fuse with them, not knowing where he leaves off and others begin. This lack of firm boundaries will be a recurring problem in marriage."(p.18)

All marriages are haunted by ghosts of the past. We are complex people who carry many and varied life experiences into our marriage. Every marriage finds itself adapting to developmental changes in our spouse. Every marriage faces the redefinition each of us goes through as we deal with our psychological history. Healthy marriages live with a respect for the complexity of our individual personalities, including understanding how childhood experiences affect the relationship.

In order to fully examine and understand my own psychological history, I turned to professional counselors, which may or may not be necessary for you. Some people need extensive therapy. Many do not need counseling in order to examine their past. There are things we can do on our own in order to understand how our childhood has shaped our personality. The purpose of this chapter is to assist in this process.

I have made a few changes in my personality as a result of examining my psychological history. These changes have come slowly and over many years. But the primary purpose of examining our childhood is not in order to bring about change or solve a problem. The purpose is to bring us closer to our spouse amidst differences.

Little children constantly seek approval. For a child, approval is experienced as love. Parents naturally disapprove when a child acts in ways that are undesirable and wrong. At a young age children view disapproval as conditional love. Disapproval plants seeds of self-doubt. A message is received by the child that he/she is not loved the way they are. The disapproval comes in the form of an irritating look, scolding, threats and physical punishment. Children will tailor their behavior as they respond to disapproval. These feelings and behavior patterns are carried into a marriage.

It is an interesting reality. Children feel secure when rules and discipline are used to teach right and wrong. At the same time, the fear and disapproval that accompany rules and discipline leave children with a degree of insecurity.

I remember when my two-year-old walked across the street to play. I had told him he must never go across the street by himself. My intent was to instill some fear and guilt into him. Even though it communicated a degree of conditional love, I knew it was for his own good. This life event communicated to my son that I would love him *if* he did what I expected. Understanding how conditional love comes through childhood experiences is power for dealing with our insecurities and growing a strong marriage.

Children lack the emotional and intellectual base of experience to know whether their parents' ideas, values and messages are correct. For example, if a young girl is told by her mother that men can't be trusted, we can expect such a message to impact the girl's relationship with her husband. If a young boy's father believes women are the weaker sex and treats his wife disrespectfully, we can expect this to impact the boy's relationship with his wife.

We tend to bring unmet childhood needs into our marriage. Sometimes a spouse is expected to make up for the love their partner did not receive from his/her parents.

Our adult personality and, therefore, our marriages are affected by childhood experiences of rejection, being ignored, criticized, neglected or smothered. This is often outside our awareness. This reality emphasizes the need for bringing our psychological history to our conscious awareness.

Now let me offer a word of caution. It is counterproductive to blame parents for who we are today. Our parents were doing the best job they knew how. All parents make mistakes. All of us did and said things that have negative impact on our adult children. Blaming only slows the process of self-examination and hinders personal growth. We are called to take responsibility for who we are. Rather than blaming parents, examine your family of origin and learn from the information. This includes recognizing and affirming the positive aspects of your parents and how they raised you.

While it is important that we not blame our parents for things in the past, it would behoove those of us who are parents to take a close look at our motivation for what we do and say to our kids. What is our motivation behind teaching children morals? Although parental expectations are essential for raising emotionally healthy children, parents can examine carefully their motivation for establishing rules and discipline. Parents are sometimes motivated by what is the convenient and expedient way to get what they want and expect from children. Even small children sense the difference between being asked to do something because it is right and good rather than because it is expedient and for the parent's convenience.

Examining the impact parents have upon our personality also includes examining our own parent's psychological history. I recall the time in my life when I stopped blaming my father. I had spent more time and energy than I would like to admit blaming my father for some parts of my personality that were, in my judgment, unhealthy. The change came when my counselor helped me get in touch with a significant part of my father's past. When my dad was in the eighth grade, his father got into trouble and was sent to prison. Through a somewhat painful but redemptive process, the counselor helped me understand the feelings my father carried into adulthood as a result of this experience. I was able to understand why he did and said some things that I felt had a negative impact on certain parts of my personality.

I have also talked with many others who have struggled with reconciling their pasts. One woman named Marie was one of them. This married mother of three children came to me for counseling. She began by telling me how upset she was with her mother. "My mother is so critical of me. She criticizes me about my house, how I discipline the children, how I prioritize my time, and a lot more. I can't stand it. What do you suggest I do?" I responded, "Do you like history?" She replied, "Actually, I was very good at history in school. Yes, I like history." I continued. "It appears that you have not done your history homework." "What do you mean?", she asked. I proceeded to share the information about how learning more about my father's history helped me to deal with some of my issues. After several sessions of examining her mother's psychological history, Marie began to realize there was nothing she could do or say that would change her mother from being critical. Understanding her mother's history freed Marie to focus on how she was responding to the criticism. With new insights about her mother and with time, Marie was able to let the criticism come and go without reacting so strongly.

Within each of us is a built-in emotional tape recorder. That tape recorder is filled with a variety of messages. These messages are placed on the recorder from the day we are born. They are simply part of growing up.

Most of the messages came from our parents. Many of the messages were verbal. Some were non-verbal, such as a look or sigh. The messages are about how we should or should not act or think in any given situation. Sometimes the messages came in the form of praise and approval and sometimes with criticism and disapproval. Some of the message came via an event. Some of those events may have been traumatic. In most cases, it is easier to identify messages that come as a result of a traumatic event rather than the ordinary experiences.

The nature of the messages is not as important as what we do with the message. Childhood messages cannot be erased from our internal tape recorder. As adults we have the capabilities of updating the messages with more adult-type information, especially when a message is not helpful.

When we received these messages as children, the normal response was to be compliant. Sometimes we responded to the message by being defiant. It is no secret that our parents preferred compliance to rebellion. Good things happened when we complied with the expectations of our parents. It is important to understand that our compliance often included a degree of guilt and fear. We carry these feelings of insecurity into our marriage.

Every day we respond to a variety of issues and situations. When this happens, our emotional tape recorder automatically begins playing a childhood message that tells us how we should or should not respond. We can choose to respond to the message as a child, or we can decide to respond in a manner that makes sense to our adult mind.

Here are examples of life experiences that are accompanied by messages recorded on our inner tape recorder: intelligence, role expectations of males and females, sex, money, external appearance, selfishness, being responsible, being angry, being good enough, work, play, use of time, trying, achieving, religion, being prompt, expressing feelings, success, failure, morality.

Each of these categories is communicated to a child with words such as, you should, should not, you need to, you ought, you must and you can or cannot.

Ask your spouse to join you in adding to this list. Be specific on the nature of the message and how the message came to you, for example, verbally, non-verbally or through an event. What messages have been recorded on your internal tape recorder? How are they played out in your marriage? Discuss how a message and/or event contributed to your self-esteem and self-image.

Here are questions that will help as you examine your psychological history.

- When and how did your parents praise you and give you approval?
- When and how did your parents criticize you and give disapproval?
- What was communicated to you (helpful or not helpful) by the way your parent approached the issue of being successful?
- How did your parents deal or not deal with conflict and anger. How has that affected how you and your spouse deal or don't deal with conflict and anger?
- List specific ways your parents expected you to measure up.
- What did you not get emotionally from your parents but wanted to get?
- What were some events in your life that enhanced or diminished your self-esteem?
- What messages do you have from your parents about being independent, and what messages do you have when your parents wanted to protect you?
- What do you perceive to be your parent's degree of self-esteem and how was that communicated to you?
- What are things you do or say that are like what your parents did and said? What are your deliberate attempts to avoid repeating what your parents did or said?
- What did your parents communicate to you about what it means to be male or female?

- Recall any sexual overtones or experiences in your home. What effect has this had on your adult life?
- What separation experiences did you have as a child, e.g. a move, divorce, death, betrayal?
- How did your parents deal with your feelings? Did your parents openly express their feelings?

Here are a few examples that may help you identify and examine your parent's messages:

Janie's parents divorced when she was very young. At the time she felt it was her fault. She carries into her marriage feelings of guilt, accompanied by an implied message that everything is her fault. Not everyone who experiences a divorce responds like Janie. A divorce may place other messages on an internal tape recorder, such as "don't be close." If someone you love and trust leaves, such as a parent, often the response is to avoid the pain of rejection by refraining from getting close to people. This may even include your spouse.

When Joan was very young her mother talked her into playing the piano at a recital. Joan did not want to perform in a recital, but her mother insisted. In the middle of her piece, Joan went blank and stopped playing. Her mother was embarrassed. She yanked Joan by her arm and pulled her out of the recital room. A message was recorded and she carries it into her marriage. The message is, don't fail. She told herself that people will be disappointed in her if she did not perform to what is expected. As an adult, with this message on her internal tape recorder, Joan was reluctant to recognize her potential. She was afraid to be successful. "You will fail" was the message she would play more often than was healthy. Her low self-esteem affected her relationship with her husband, even though he would tell her she was successful and had great potential.

Jack grew up with a father who was very strict. He was afraid of his father and felt he had to watch his every move. He felt his father loved him only if he lived up to his high expectations. His mother was very lenient. Jack could get away with anything when it came to his mother. At times he wondered if she really cared what he did. These mixed messages had a confusing effect on Jack's personality. The accompanying feelings played out in his relationship with his wife and were a source of tension in their marriage. Because he was insecure about being loved, he was very needy. His wife did not respond favorably to his neediness.

Jim's parents were not demonstrative. He rarely saw his parents show affection towards each other. Sex was never discussed. If the topic inadvertently came up, the parent's response communicated a message that sex is somehow bad or dirty. This parent tape/message had a negative impact on the lovemaking part of his marriage.

Maxine's father was a classic male chauvinist. As a little girl, Maxine would witness the many ways her father would put down her mother. Her mother would not defend herself. The message Maxine carried into her marriage was that women are inferior, stupid and powerless. In the first years of her marriage, she related to her husband just like her mother. Steve, her husband, experienced this as normal. His parents had related to each other in similar fashion, although not to the extreme of Maxine's. In time, she began to rebel. Steve could not understand why she had become so angry about what he considered to be minor things. The marriage began to fall apart.

Joseph grew up in just the opposite atmosphere, his mother dominated his father. He felt his father was weak and inept. He viewed his mother as a nag. Consequently, this is the way he saw most women. I will leave it to you to discern how the marriage was affected.

Throughout his early life, Lee heard his parents repeatedly tell him how selfish he was and how he was always thinking only of himself. He would never amount to anything unless he changed his ways. Lee recorded on his young inner tape recorder a message that said he was not important and of value.

When Kenneth was a child he would, like most small children, express feelings of mad and angry. His father would not permit any such expressions of feelings. Kenneth recorded on his tape recorder a message that said, "Don't show your feelings" and/or "don't know your feelings." As a young child, Kenneth did not distinguish between one feeling and another. Therefore, the messages he has about showing angry feelings includes other feelings such as lonely and afraid. This message affects his relationship with his wife who wants him to share his feelings.

When Teri was approximately one year old, she had a serious childhood disease. During the next five or six years she spent a considerable amount of time in doctor's offices and the hospital. Understandably, her parents and the medical community gave her lots of attention. Shortly after turning seven, the disease went into remission. The visits to the doctors and hospital stopped. Her parents were grateful and relieved. The amount of attention Teri received greatly diminished. These early years had a significant impact on Teri's personality. She carried into adulthood and marriage a message that said if she was sick she would get attention. For Teri, attention was synonymous with love. As a way to get love, Teri would become sick. It was difficult to know if the sickness was real or imagined. This neediness had a negative effect on her relationships and marriage.

Both of Nancy's parents were high achievers. They were prominent personalities in their community. Everyone knew and respected them. Consequently, Nancy put unrealistic pressure on herself and her marriage. How Nancy responded to her parents' high expectations influenced her self-esteem which in turn affected how she related to her husband.

Each of these persons brought a significant amount of insecurity into their marriages. Paradoxically, the same experiences and messages that gave them a degree of inner security also had a positive influence. Although Janie's parents divorced, they were very intentional about spending quality and quantity time with her after the divorce. Joan's mother let her know she was there for her and spent time playing games with her. Jack's father had a warm and tender side of him which gave Jack feelings of security. Maxine's father often treated her as if she were the most important person in the world and valued her as a female. Joseph's mother also let him see the vulnerable side of her. Lee's parents gave him lots of love, leaving him feeling he was important and of value. One day, two-year-old Kenneth fell, hurt his knee and cried. His father took him into his arms and comforted him. Teri's parents did not need her to be sick in order for them to love her, but that is not what Teri felt. Nancy's parents would not love her less if she did not follow in their footsteps. The point is: Messages from parents bring about both secure and insecure feelings.

I hope these illustrations will stimulate the process of exploring your own psychological history.

Each of us has a story of how our past has influenced who we are today. Your story may have some negative aspects; but it must not be viewed as negative, rather simply your story. We have the power to choose how our childhood story is lived out. Share with your spouse your childhood experiences and how they influence your personality and values.

Recently my son and I were talking about how our past affects our personalities, particularly our family of origin. He said to me, "Are you saying what you and mom did or did not do affects who I am, how I feel, think and act as an adult?" I responded, "Yes, but it's not that simple. There are many factors in addition to parents that helped form our personalities. These include TV, teachers, church, books, cultural expectations, social mores, peers, siblings and our many and varied life experiences."

For example, our personality is affected by how our society communicates certain distorted images of what constitutes an attractive body. Most of us fall short of having a physical appearance that meets society's unrealistic expectations as to what constitutes "beauty". Popularity and acceptance are artificially determined by a narrow definition of what society considers being talented. Also in our society, success is closely tied to winning. Success is being better than someone, including having more financial wealth. All of these societal norms come with messages that affect our marriage as they contribute to feelings of insecurity, low self-esteem and lack of self-worth.

Examining how birth order influences our personalities can also be helpful in understanding our psychological history. What is the dynamic that takes place when two older children marry, or an older marries a youngest, or a middle child marries an only child, etc . . . ? Books on birth order may be helpful to you. *The New Birth Order Book, Why You Are the Way You Are* by Dr. Kevin Leman and *Born to Rebel, Birth Order, Family Dynamics, and Creative Lives*, by Frank J. Sulloway.

Activate your inner power by looking closely at how you and your spouse were raised and the impact those experiences have on your marriage.

QUESTIONS FOR PERSONAL REFLECTION AND DISCUSSION WITH YOUR SPOUSE

KISS 1: Share times in your life when you have examined your psychological history. Was it a positive experience? Why, why not?

KISS 2: How has your psychological history affected your feelings of being a secure and insecure person?

KISS 3: Discuss how and why conditional love is an inevitable part of our life experiences and thus every marriage.

KISS: 4: Share with your spouse how your parent's psychological history has influenced the way you were raised.

KISS 5: What messages have been recorded on your internal tape recorder and how are they played out in your marriage.

KISS 6: What messages about sexuality affect the health of your lovemaking?

KISS 7: Has birth order affected your relationship? Why? Why not?

KISS 8: Besides your parents, how have other events of life influenced your personality?

5

Feelings: Help or Hindrance

On a recent summer evening, my wife and I were sitting on our patio soaking up a beautiful sunset and discussing the events of the day. It was wonderful until she asked, "What was your strongest feeling today?" The warmth of the beautiful sun suddenly faded as I froze.

I am a man. Discussions about feelings aren't high on my agenda.

I may have stressed the importance of sharing feelings in numerous marriage and counseling sessions, but I still have trouble sharing my own feelings.

Evidently, I am not alone in my phobia of feelings. I have had numerous women say to me, "My husband doesn't share his feelings with me." Studies show that, in general, women use many more words in a day than their men counterparts. However, I am not convinced that women are much better than men at identifying and sharing their feelings. They may be better at showing emotion when they are talking about their feelings, but there's more to it than that.

Feelings are a fundamental part of our life and relationships. Feelings connect us to what is really important in our marriage. When identified, understood and shared, feelings become a source of power for addressing the many issues of marriage. When feelings are not identified, understood and shared, communication is impaired and tensions are escalated.

Our feelings have great power. Feelings can be extremely helpful or become a hindrance. Feelings can be the basis of happiness or unhappiness. Feelings can increase love or obstruct love. Feelings can open doors to what is possible or can block access to what is important to us.

Understanding the following six factors will contribute to feelings becoming a help and not a hindrance:

I.   Recognize that sharing a *thought* is different than sharing a *feeling*.

If you had known Elaine and me after seven or eight years of marriage and asked, "How is your marriage?" the answer would have been, "Fine. We are doing OK." "How is your communication?" "Our communication is great. There isn't anything we can't talk about. We are completely open and honest with each other about any and every topic."

Then, our eyes were opened at a marriage retreat. We were surprised to learn we were good at communicating our thoughts, but lousy at communicating our feelings. More importantly, we did not understand the difference between a thought and a feeling. I have found this to be the case with most marriages.

We were expressing a thought to each other and assuming that we were expressing a feeling. The thought may have been expressed with emotion and intensity, but that didn't mean we knew what the other was feeling. Learning the difference between a thought and a feeling has been a major source for strengthening our love and dealing with disagreements.

Here are some suggestions on how to distinguish between a thought and a feeling:

- Beginning a sentence with "I feel" does not guarantee you have shared a feeling. You have conveyed a thought when you follow "I feel" with the words "like" or "that." For example, a person might say, "I feel anxious when you forget to follow up on our plan." This sentence is expressing a feeling, "anxious." Now insert the word "like" or "that" after the word "feel". It does not make sense and is a hint you are expressing a thought not a feeling. "I feel that/like you will forget to follow up on our plan" expresses a thought, but not the "anxious" feeling.

- If you can substitute "I am" for "I feel", you have expressed a feeling. For example, *I am* scared when I think of the future. *I feel* scared when I think of the future. If you can substitute "I think" for "I feel" you have expressed a thought. For example, I feel we should paint the house is not expressing a feeling if I can also say, I think we should paint the house. The difference between a thought and a feeling can be seen in this sentence: "When I think about painting the house I feel overwhelmed."

II. Learn those four little words.

I have found there are four words that sum up all of the feelings I consider vulnerable and uncomfortable: **lonely, scared, guilt** and **anger.**

When someone is experiencing difficulty in their life, they often say they feel "bad" or "hurt." Those two words are too general to express someone's true feelings. It doesn't sufficiently communicate what is going on inside of a person. Even descriptions such as "embarrassed" or "worried" are too general. When we are experiencing these emotions we might actually be feeling guilt, fear or anger, maybe even loneliness.

One couple came in for counseling after the husband, Max, had received notice of a possible job change. He felt it was a wonderful opportunity, even though it meant moving to another state. His wife, Maggie, felt strongly about staying put. They had talked about the issue over and over and each time the conversation ended in anger.

Maggie wanted to begin our session by telling me how she felt about the impending move. She quickly explained the reasons she did not want to move. Max had heard these reasons many times, just as she had heard his reasons for wanting to take the new job. Again, they had shared their thoughts but not their feelings.

When I invited Maggie to get in touch with her feelings she finally said, "I feel unimportant." I asked what her six-year-old daughter would say if she was feeling unimportant. Maggie thought for a moment and said, "She would probably say she feels scared." I asked her to finish this sentence: "When I tell myself I am unimportant to Max I feel . . ." She responded, "I feel lonely."

Maggie had given her husband all of the reasons not to leave, but she had failed to communicate to him that she was feeling scared and lonely. I did a similar exercise with Max, and he also was able to identify that he was also feeling scared and lonely.

Max and Maggie did something that can be useful when trying to pinpoint our feelings. They went back to their six-year-old selves and tried to remember how they would have described their feelings. This process boils down feelings so that you can express them.

In one of our marriage workshops someone asked, "You said most feelings can be summarized in four words. This is fine; but if I am to begin sharing feelings with my wife, I need some help in knowing some feeling words." On my computer, I googled "List of Feelings". I told my friend to do the same. What comes up is a multitude of options for feeling words. Try it.

III. It is all in the details.

Learning how to *describe* a feeling will help our spouse understand what we are feeling.

One way to describe a feeling is by referring to an event or experience. For example, when you are feeling scared you might say it is like the time I was separated from my parents at the mall, or the time I heard my parents had been in a car wreck. If I were feeling guilty, I may describe it by referring to the time I lied to my parents about who broke the window. If I am feeling lonely I might describe it by saying it is like the time I spent four hours in jail.

Another way of describing a feeling is to indicate the intensity. For example, on a scale of one to ten, I feel like a nine.

Then there are people who use the four senses to describe a feeling. If a feeling is good they might say the feeling is like *hearing* four professional violinists play a song in unison, *tasting* cold water on a hot summer day, *touching* a newborn baby or *smelling* freshly baked bread.

If it is a bad feeling, they may describe the feeling as *hearing* a song played on a piano that has not been tuned for 25 years, *touching* a dead animal or *smelling* a rotten banana.

How you describe your feelings is up to you. But remember, your partner cannot get inside your head, doesn't share your same life experiences and may need more information about your feelings in order to truly understand.

IV. Control issues

Many of us resist sharing our feelings for one reason; we want to be in control. We learned the importance of being in control very early in life.

In some families, expressing difficult and uncomfortable feelings indicated a person was out of control. As children, we got the message that being in control was a good thing. Being out of control was not a good thing.

I spent a considerable amount of time helping Rex understand the importance of sharing feelings with his wife and how to go about it. Finally, he said to me, "I understand what you are saying. I'm no dummy. But I find myself reluctant to share my feelings with her." When we got down to it, he felt as if he were losing some of his control when he shared too much.

Being reluctant to share our feelings comes from the natural tendency to avoid pain. All of us want to control pain. Although sharing feelings enhances closeness, being vulnerable also carries with it a degree of emotional pain.

We try to control the amount of pain in our life by avoiding conflict with our spouse. By not sharing feelings, we convince ourselves that we can avoid conflict or at least avoid making the conflict so intense. Why share feelings when we know it is only going to upset our spouse and create an unpleasant situation? I remember one man said to me, "Sharing feelings only creates more tension in our marriage."

We frequently have a need to protect our spouse from the pain and conflict that may result from sharing our feelings. But consider the consequence of protecting your spouse. The pain may be avoided for awhile, but only for awhile. Suppressed feelings are bound to come out sooner or later and often in unhealthy ways.

In the workplace, being in control is valued. At work, clear thinking and decisive action are important for success. Freely expressing feelings at work is generally not looked upon as an admirable trait of a competent employee or boss. You are praised and rewarded for fixing and solving problems.

Contrast this with the experience of walking into the house at the end of the work day to find that feelings are valued. Fixing our spouse and solving a problem take second place to sharing of feelings. Dealing with feelings does not carry with it the amount of control that is expected at work.

Add to all of this that when something happens to generate a feeling, rarely is it just one feeling. Most of the time our response is a combination of several feelings. It is very difficult to be in control of one feeling. It is even more problematical to be in control as we experience a minefield of feelings and emotions. We may tell ourselves we can retain a degree of control over our lives by avoiding the complexity of our feelings.

Then there is the whole matter of the unknown. There is risk in sharing feelings. There is no guarantee that sharing feelings with your spouse will enhance your married love. Maybe we can control the unknown by not sharing our feelings.

Share with your spouse how these control issues affect your relationship.

V. It all goes back to the beginning.

Reluctance to knowing and showing feelings may have roots in the messages you received from your parents in every day situations.

Here are just a few statements children often hear. Say each one out loud. Ask yourself whether the statement communicates to a child that feelings are to be avoided or, at least, not openly expressed:

- There is no place for that kind of thing.
- It's no big deal. Why are you so upset?
- It's over. Let it go.
- Don't cry over spilt milk.
- Nothing is accomplished by looking back.
- It's not really that important.
- Don't be so selfish.
- Don't make a mountain out of a molehill.
- It's a waste of energy to get so upset.
- Cheer up. It's going to be OK.
- You shouldn't feel that way.
- You don't really hate your sister, do you?
- You're just saying that because you are so tired.
- Don't talk that way.
- You know you don't mean that.
- That is a terrible thing to say.
- Stop that crying
- You have blown things out of proportion.
- Don't take things so personally.

I'm sure that you can add to this list. Sometimes the words are very subtle; but as a child we hear the message: "Don't express your feelings."

The "don't express feelings" message may have come nonverbally. For example, I have a clear recollection of a time when I saw my father cry. I was in the fourth grade. It was the only time I saw him cry. And I never saw my mother cry, not even at my father's funeral. The message I got as a small child was not to show my feelings. I am sure my parents cried, but not in front of me. I never saw my parents' guilt, fear or loneliness expressed. I did see their anger. I suspect they grew up in a home with "don't express feelings" messages. Or they might have believed it was best to protect us by not showing their feelings.

In general, women are more willing to talk about their feelings. However, in order to not seem like a whiney, women may talk more about what is going on in their life; but also avoid dealing with feelings, their own or their husbands.

I have taken into adulthood and marriage a message that says it is best to keep my feelings inside and not show them. This seems to be especially true for young boys. Feelings are a sign of weakness. Be strong. Therefore, when I am in a movie and feel like crying, I try hard to hold back. Big boys don't cry. I am a man.

For some, sharing feelings is associated with being viewed as inferior or weak. One way to cope and defend against these discouraging self-images is to deny feeling what we feel.

The repression of feelings can even go a step further. Even if we do know what we feel, do we let the feeling show?

Think back to your childhood. Did you have permission as a young child to express anger openly towards your parents without being reprimanded? Most of us were probably told to go to our room until we could learn to control our anger. It was then in childhood that we made the unconscious decision to control our feelings. We take that message into a marriage.

VI. Feeling unhealthy

It's well documented in the medical and psychiatric communities that many physical and emotional sicknesses are the direct result of unexpressed feelings.

If you are not convinced of this, here is an exercise that illustrates what happens in your body when feelings are stored-up. Hold out your arm. Now roll up your fingers into a ball and squeeze as tight as you can. Hold that for five minutes or fifteen minutes. What would happen if you held it for one hour? Your whole body would be negatively affected. Do you get the point of what happens to your body when your feelings are not expressed? The balled up fist is just like the ball of feelings inside of us when they aren't expressed.

When feelings are stored up we feel physically and emotionally sick. Remember as a child when you had a stomach ache and vomited? Two good things happened when you threw up. First you felt better. Second, someone cleaned it up for you.

When stored-up feelings are shared in a marriage, two good things happen. First, we feel better. Second, our lover is there to clean it up if we are willing to share our feelings and our spouse is willing to listen to our feelings and not give advice. Some people are fortunate enough to have a friend who is willing to clean up the dregs of expressed feelings. Hopefully, your spouse is that kind of friend.

Unexpressed feelings, in time, will come out in subtle ways. When the stored-up feelings finally emerge, the consequences are often neither healthy nor helpful. Stored-up feelings are a major source of depression. Depressed people have difficulty communicating.

Many people are telling us how certain food negatively affects our bodies. Feelings are the health food of marriage. Barbara DeAngelis in her helpful book, *How To Make Love All The Time*, says, "Just as your nerves report physical sensations to help keep you safe physically, so your feelings tune you in to what you need for emotional health." (p. 113)

Stored-up feelings are a barrier to healthy communication. When couples verbalize their feelings to each other, it may cause some tension. When couples do *not* verbalize their feelings, you can predict there will be an even greater amount of tension. You have heard the saying, "What you feel you can heal."

Sharing feelings is one of the best ways to express love. Conversely, withholding feelings is a way of withholding love. Trust is built through sharing feelings. When we share feelings we say to our spouse, "I trust you can handle my feelings."

Shared feelings bring to a marriage excitement and fulfillment. All of us have experienced a degree of monotony and even some boredom with the daily routine of marriage. Reporting to our spouse about what happened during the day can also feel repetitious and dull. But sharing what you felt during the day brings newness to the conversation. Shared feelings bring stimulation and passion to the conversation and relationship. When couples share their feelings, not just their thoughts, ordinary events of the day become special moments that give depth and richness to life and love.

"I'm a positive person. I don't like to extend the kind of negative energy that comes with sharing difficult and uncomfortable feelings. I like to share positive feelings with my spouse, but not negative feelings." This philosophy may also come from our upbringing as well as society. Is this philosophy just a way to avoid knowing and showing feelings?

Jim and Jill's experience reveal the issues that come up when talking about feelings. When they came for counseling, they were unclear on the exact nature of the problem. "We seldom fight," said Jill. "We just don't connect. I guess it is a matter of communication." I continued asking them to share what was going on until finally Jill said, "We don't talk about anything important. Jim just doesn't share his feelings." It didn't take me long to find out that while Jill talked more, she was not much better than Jim when it came to sharing feelings.

I asked Jim whether he thought Jill was right about not sharing his feelings. Jim responded, "Yea, I've always been sort of a private person. I never saw my parents share feelings. Besides, I think we avoid a lot of bickering by not sharing feelings."

I quickly realized that Jim and Jill did not understand the difference between sharing a thought and sharing a feeling. With Jill present in the room, I began to work with Jim. It did not take long for him to open up and share his feelings. The main feeling he identified was loneliness. His job was filled with pressure. He had not shared how he felt about his job, thinking that he needed to protect Jill from all the confusion and conflict surrounding his job.

When he had finished sharing, I asked Jill for her response to hearing her husband share his lonely feeling. Jill said, "I am not sure how I feel, and I don't know why I don't know." After some thought, she reported it was because of their history together. For most of their marriage, he had not shared his feelings. Why should she trust it now?

I continued to pursue her feelings when her husband shared his lonely feelings. She began to realize that, although she talked more than Jim about issues, she also had difficulty identifying and sharing her feelings. In addition to mistrust, she was angry. Why? For most of her marriage, she felt left out of his life because he did not share his feelings. She resented having to live this way for so long.

I pursued other feelings she might be having. With a little prodding, she said she felt scared. I asked her to explain. She was, at first, a little surprised she was feeling scared. Then she realized it had to do with her own insecure feelings. She looked to her husband to be strong. His being strong was important, especially when she often felt insecure about her life and future. It also was a matter of control. She did not like him to control her. At the same time, when he shared his feeling, she felt he was not in control. Jill realized she needed help in seeing him as strong even though he had insecure feelings.

I turned to Jim and asked how he felt about Jill's response. As I expected, he said that he felt even more lonely and scared. How was he to be strong and at the same time share his vulnerable self?

Doris and Dave had a different experience. Dave admitted he was reluctant to share feelings with Doris. Doris viewed her husband as smart, strong and capable. In Doris's presence, I helped Dave open up and share some of his feelings. I then turned to Doris and asked, "How are you responding when Dave shares his feelings?" Her silence indicated she wanted to give my questions serious consideration. Finally, she said, "I feel I can trust that he is committed to making our marriage healthy." Dave was somewhat surprised at his wife's response. Would sharing feelings indicate to her that he was inadequate and weak rather than smart and strong? He was relieved. Although he did not begin to express his feelings with abandonment, a new freedom and closeness began to emerge in their marriage.

Until we are proficient at something, doing it is hard work. This is especially true of sharing feelings. Sharing *thoughts* does not require the same amount of effort and attention as sharing feelings. Sharing feelings carries with it risk and hard work.

I hope this chapter on feelings will help you become adept at identifying, understanding, and sharing feelings with your spouse. I am still learning how to express my feelings to Elaine. There is a learning curve. It takes time and practice. Sharing feelings with your spouse will free you and your spouse to make love a more fulfilling part of your life.

QUESTIONS FOR PERSONAL REFLECTION
AND
DISCUSSION WITH YOUR SPOUSE

KISS 1: Discuss the author's distinction between sharing a thought and sharing a feeling. Why do you agree or disagree that the distinction is important for communication in a marriage?

KISS 2: Identify an uncomfortable feeling word. Consider how that word could be replaced with lonely, guilt, fear or anger.

KISS 3: Choose a feeling word, one you might use when you feel insecure and vulnerable. Try your hand at describing that feeling to your spouse.

KISS 4: Identify and share with your spouse childhood messages that hinder you from freely expressing your feelings.

KISS 5: On a scale of one to ten, how proficient are you in expressing your feelings? Using the same scale, how do you evaluate your spouse? Share your answers and discuss any differences.

KISS 6: Share a time when you shared your lonely, guilty or scared feelings with your spouse. Shares a time when you recall your spouse shared his/her lonely, guilty or scared feelings with you.

6

Fighting the Good Fight

What do you mean, "good" fight? Yes, there are good and bad fights. There are constructive and destructive ways of expressing anger to our spouse.

In premarital counseling, I ask couples to describe their fighting style. Most couples respond with a blank look and are quick to tell me they do not fight. They admit to having disagreements but say they talk things out rationally.

Being rational is important in any relationship, but being rational when we are angry is an unrealistic expectation. It is that expectation that causes many fights to turn from the "good" kind to the "bad" kind.

Adriana came to me for counseling. In the past several months, she noticed she was getting increasingly angry with her husband of ten years. She was feeling guilty about her angry feelings because she truly loved her husband. After she explained her situation, I asked her, "What do you want from me?" "I want to stop being angry. It isn't helpful to our relationship, and I haven't been angry with him in the past." I responded, "You don't want to get angry at your husband? Do I hear you correctly" "Yes", she answered. I said, "I can't help you." She stared at me with a questioning look and said, "But I was sure you could help me."

I went on to explain that the reason I couldn't help her stop the anger was because it is a normal emotion in marriage. She probably had felt angry at her husband long before the last several months but had suppressed it. Helping her understand that being angry is normal gave her the permission she needed. The permission enabled her to lessen her feelings of guilt and begin learning how to fight constructively with her spouse.

In every marriage book I have read, there is a chapter on conflict and anger. In my judgment, some of the suggestions contradict my assertion that anger is normal in a marriage. For example, one author talks about how to express differences without arguing. He writes, "As a basic guideline, never argue. Instead, discuss the pros and cons of something. Negotiate for what you want but don't argue." This sounds similar to the suggestion that instead of fighting, talk out your differences in a rational manner. This advice is not realistic. It also avoids the diligent work required for learning how to express anger in ways that are constructive.

There are many other published suggestions for fighting fairly in your marriage that seem unrealistic:

a. Disagree but do not be disagreeable.
b. Do not bring up the past.
c. Listen to the other's point of view.
d. Learn to soothe yourself. Be calm. Talk intelligently and rationally.
e. Hold hands when fighting.
f. Do not use harsh words.
g. When your spouse attacks you verbally, do not get defensive.
h. In your fighting set a time for recess/intermission.
i. Limit the fight to 15 minutes. Set a timer.

If any of these suggestions work for your marriage, do them. But as a counselor and after 49 years of marriage it has been my experience that these suggestions will not work for the long-term. They will eventually prove to be impractical and sterile.

Then there are some who say that fighting is the result of a breakdown in communication. This is like saying if everyone in the world spoke the same language there would be no wars. Good communication skills do not keep us from having the normal and inevitable feeling of anger. Learning how to effectively "do" anger in a marriage is different from learning communication skills.

Some suggest an important part of conflict is compromising. For Elaine and me compromise has rarely been helpful. All too often, compromise means someone has given in. Initially, compromise may be viewed as a way of easing the conflict. Look carefully at the value of compromise, especially if compromise means sacrificing your beliefs and not being true to yourself. The "peace at any price" approach may ease the conflict for awhile. But very soon resentment will emerge and may even make the situation worse.

I disagree with the idea by some that a "bad" fight is fighting without ever coming to a resolution. Do not expect learning how to express anger to result in a resolution of the issue that precipitated the anger.

When Elaine and I fight, it is usually about inconsequential things and the result of our fragile egos working overtime. The rest of the time, our anger is about issues that are not solvable. Our differences run too deep. In fact, our fights have become fewer and less intense since we realized that the purpose of fighting is not to solve an issue or to get our partner to change. Trying to change your spouse is an exercise in futility. We certainly cannot expect change to come through expressing anger.

So what is the purpose of fighting? Other than doing something normal couples do from time to time and keeping the marriage strong, does fighting need to have a purpose?

Although fighting and anger in marriage are normal, what is deemed normal may vary from couple to couple. Intensity and frequency of the anger are the usual criteria most couples use to define what is normal for their marriage. I know some couples who fight frequently and intensely and have a good marriage. Likewise, I know marriages that are in trouble although their anger and fights are not as intense and frequent.

I think there are abnormal ways to express anger. Partners need to share what they consider to be abnormal in their marriage. Your definition of *abnormal* may vary from that of another couple. For Elaine and me, physically hitting is abnormal. We also have decided certain words are off limits and come under the category of abnormal.

There have been times when I was so angry at my wife that I told myself being divorced would be better. Throughout the many years of sharing love with Elaine, I have grown to realize my feelings of anger are normal. It is freeing to expect I will have angry feelings even though, at the time, it felt like the anger would never pass. Sometimes it takes only a few minutes for my anger to pass. Sometimes it takes a few hours and, in rare occasions, a few days. This has come through trial and lots of error. More importantly, it has come through learning how to fight and express anger. The key words are *learning* and *how*.

One author writes that "anger is destructive to a relationship no matter what form it takes." I disagree. The form anger and fighting takes determines whether it is destructive or constructive. It is crucial for couples to decide intentionally what form fighting will take in their marriage, even though, when the actual fight happens, a couple may not adhere to the predefined form they have chosen.

You may not think it does any good to get mad, but I say yes it does when the mad and fighting are done in a way that increases love. It was helpful to Elaine and me to discover that *how* we fought, i.e. our method/form of fighting, was not what we wanted and did not make sense. We continue to get angry and fight, but our focus is on *how* to do it in a way that is more constructive than destructive.

Most people do not feel loving when they are angry, but the method/form/pattern of fighting is a loving decision. Learning how to express anger and fight insures that closeness and love remain strong even amidst fights and anger.

Eight Steps for Constructive Fighting

STEP ONE: *Carefully examine the messages about anger you received or didn't receive from your parents.*

The messages may have come through their actions. The messages about anger may have come verbally or nonverbally. What did you see when your parents got angry? How did they deal or not deal with their anger? How did they respond to your anger? What message did you receive when they responded to your anger?

Step one helps us confront the fact that few of us were taught it is all right to be angry. Therefore, we grow up thinking it is wrong to express anger. As a child, when we were forming how we should or should not feel, some children had permission to know they were angry, but certainly not show the anger. For most of us, expressing anger as a child was unacceptable to our parents or, at least, we were taught to control our anger.

Ask yourself whether you had permission to openly express anger to your parents without being reprimanded. "I don't want to hear you say that ever again." "I'll have none of that back talk." "Don't talk to me like that." If we talked to our parents with anger, the consequences were not good ones. Even angry looks were forbidden. A teenager who slams the bedroom door in rage is forced to apologize and is punished. Therefore, very early in life, we learned to avoid expressing anger openly and honestly.

We may or may not have seen our parents angry. How our parents did or did not model expressions of anger has a degree of influence on how we express anger in our marriage. We carry this pattern into our marriage. It is helpful for couples to discuss whether the patterns of anger learned as a child are healthy for their marriage. When we are feeling anger, step one is a way to begin breaking unhealthy patterns.

You may also have received a message about expressing anger from other sources, such as the church. Name and evaluate these messages.

STEP TWO: *When you are mad at your spouse, say out loud, "I am angry at you."*

Until we can name and claim our anger it is unlikely that we will deal with anger in a constructive and healthy manner. Saying the sentence in your mind will not have the same effect as saying it out loud. Although saying this sentence to your spouse could be a powerful tool for dealing with anger, telling yourself you are feeling anger is even more important. Saying out loud, "I am angry at you", enables us to face up to the tendency to avoid and deny we are angry.

By avoiding the use of the word, angry, we tell ourselves we can steer clear of something that is bad and wrong. For many, the word "anger" is too strong so we look for other words. We will use words such as disappointed, annoyed, upset, disturbed, irritated, offended, resentful, peeved, muffed and bothered. I have known individuals who say they are sad when they are feeling angry. Saying out loud, "I am angry", is an important step for dealing with anger in a direct and healthy manner.

Rather than avoid and suppress anger, should we let it all out? Is it good to vent our anger? Step two is not intended to encourage the venting of anger. I do not recommend either suppression or venting. Venting results in hurt that is unnecessary and unhealthy. Anger does not disappear when we suppress it. The angry feelings are stored up and are destined to come out later in ways that only make matters worse. In fact, some experts contend that depression is suppressed anger.

I simply recommend that an important step for dealing with anger and fighting in a marriage begins by being honest with yourself about your feelings. When we name and claim a feeling, we are more likely to deal with it in a constructive manner.

Step Three: *Say out loud: "I am **deciding** to be angry at you." The purpose of this step is three-fold.*

First, this sentence is the same as step two, but adds the word, "deciding."

Inserting the word "deciding" makes step two forceful and persuasive.

When we are not feeling well and go to the doctor, he/she may prescribe a pill. This sentence is like a pill. Obviously, a pill isn't effective until you swallow it. Likewise, this pill/sentence does not have the desired effect unless you say it out loud.

People will say to me, "I don't decide to be angry. I am just angry. I can't help it. She/he *made* me angry." Remember the point made in chapter three: nobody can make you feel something. We decide to feel what we feel.

For example, do you feel angry when someone calls you a derogatory or nasty name? The answer is: it depends. Depends, upon what? It depends upon your decision. For example, you decide whether the person meant it. How do you know if they meant it or whether they were kidding? They may tell you they were kidding, but you may or may not believe them, again, depending upon . . . it comes down to what you decide.

Some time ago, our family was playing a game of cards called Hearts. I gave my son the queen of spades and he called me an idiot. Did I get mad? I laughed, but I could have decided to get mad. Indeed, in another setting, if my son called me an idiot, I might have gotten mad. In other words, we decide how we are going to feel. It is our choice to respond to a certain event with feelings of hurt and anger.

When someone physically harms us, puts us down or calls us a name, it is difficult to refrain from feeling angry. Nevertheless, how we respond is a decision.

Saying the sentence, I am deciding to feel angry, insures that we keep our power, the power to decide how we are going to respond to any given situation. To say, "You *make* me mad", is giving your power away to that person. If you believe someone can *make* you feel something, you are giving them power over your feelings. You must wait until they change their behavior or words before you can feel differently.

Sometimes I will wait to say the sentence out loud until after Elaine and I have separated from each other because I know it will lessen the degree of my anger. Sometimes I want to be angry. I don't want my anger to subside. But when I don't want my anger to get out of control or hurt someone, it works to say this sentence out loud. It reduces both the intensity and duration of my anger.

Use this "pill" when you are angry at your spouse. I think you will like what it does for you and also for your spouse. Again, don't expect the sentence to get rid of your anger. It is one way to increase the possibility of dealing with your anger in a constructive manner.

Step three will activate the smart part of you. When we are angry we do not think clearly. Clear thinking is critical for dealing with complex relationships and situations. Our intelligence gets plugged in, and our anger is diminished when we tell ourselves we are "deciding" to be angry. We are more likely to see positive options when we are thinking clearly. We are able to keep the difficult situation in proper perspective.

I have also found this "pill" to be effective when dealing with my children. Sometimes I get so mad at a child and know I need to curtail it. So I will say to my child, "When you do that, I am deciding to be angry at you." How do you imagine a child will respond when a parent says this? In my experience the child is less threatened and fearful of my anger. More importantly, I find my anger towards my child is not as intense.

STEP Four: *Identify what you say or do not say, do or do not do when you are angry at your spouse.*

If you had met Elaine and me after eight years of marriage and asked, "Do you have fights?" I would have said, "No, we never fight." You might say, "Isn't that wonderful. You never get angry with each other." "That's not what was asked. We get angry, but we do not fight." "That is great. How do you achieve that?" We did not have fights because when the fight began I would walk away. No fighting. I thought walking away was great, only to find out it was having an adverse effect upon our marriage. Through counseling, we uncovered that we had a lot of work to do in the area of anger and fighting. We needed to look closely at the way we were doing anger with each other, i.e. identify our pattern.

How do you and your spouse fight and express anger? In order to identify your pattern, as an individual and as a couple, answer the following four questions:

Question One: If I saw you get angry at your spouse, what would I see or not see, hear or not hear? How would I know you are angry? How do you express anger to your spouse? What is your pattern? One pattern is not better than another. The key is naming the pattern of expressing anger to your spouse.

Question Two: Do you like your pattern? Yes, no, or sometimes. The question is not whether you like anger. Nobody likes anger. The question is whether you like your pattern as defined in question one.

Question Three: What is your spouse's pattern of expressing anger to you? Again, what do you see or not see, hear or not hear.

Question Four: Do you like your spouse's pattern of fighting and expressing anger?

If both of you answer questions two and four in the affirmative, your pattern for fighting and expressing anger is set, at least for now. Your pattern may change from time to time throughout your married life. If one spouse does not like the other's pattern, the question for your spouse will be: how would you prefer I fight and express anger? When your spouse tells you a preferred pattern, you can decide if you want to make the suggested changes. If you do not want to change, then your spouse must learn to adjust to a pattern he/she does not like. If your spouse doesn't want to adjust he/she can either continue unnecessary hurt or get a divorce.

Before Elaine and I got help changing our anger patterns, here is how I answered the four questions:

1. When I got angry I would walk away, get my thoughts together and come back later to finish the conversation in a "rational" manner.

Sometimes I would just let it drop and not feel a need to return to Elaine or the issue.

2. Yes, I like my pattern. There was anger but no fights.
3. I saw Elaine's pattern as wanting to continue the argument until there was a solution.
4. I did not like her pattern because most of the issues we fight about are either inconsequential or unsolvable.

Here is how Elaine answered the four questions:

1. I want to continue until there is some solution.
2. Yes, I like my pattern. We need to solve the issue and not continue fighting about it.
3. Virgil walks away and may or may not return to continue the discussion.
4. No, I do not like his pattern. When he walks away I feel lonely and scared.

When I heard Elaine did not like my pattern of walking away, the counselor asked me what I would rather do. I had no idea.

My pattern started forming when I watched my father get angry at my mother. I thought he had a good thing going for him because it avoided what I considered unnecessary fighting.

However, I did not want my wife feeling lonely and scared. I began working at not walking away. When I got angry, I would express my anger to her directly.

This new pattern worked for a while. But in time, Elaine did not like me directly giving her my anger. She began to walk away from me. I told her I did not like her walking away. She said she wanted to leave and return when she had some time to cool off. She was not willing to change her pattern to what I wanted. Therefore, I had to adjust to her pattern. You can see that our pattern of anger and fighting is still a work in progress. We continue talking about our pattern and searching for a pattern that makes sense to us and is not destructive to our love.

About three months, ago I got angry and walked away from Elaine. I had not chosen this pattern for a long time. We were in the living room and had just finished our evening devotions. In reflecting on what we had read, Elaine made a comment that felt very hurtful. I paused for about five seconds and then left the room. I remained mad for a couple of days before I came back and said I was ready to talk.

The issue was one that had been present in our relationship since the beginning. We had dealt with it many times and seemed to have adjusted. As we got older, it began to re-emerge. We decided to see our counselor and get some perspective since walking away for undecided amounts of time was hurtful to both of us. We decided the rule would be that not more than 48 hours would go by before the one who walked away would initiate talking about the issue.

There is no such thing as healthy or unhealthy anger, but there are healthy and unhealthy patterns of fighting. Making an intentional decision about how you want to fight and express anger is an important step. By doing this you are insuring that your fights do not get in the way of married love.

I challenge you to begin cultivating a pattern of fighting that works for your relationship. Be patient with any changes in your pattern that need to happen. You and your spouse may revert to the old pattern from time to time. Yes, you will not be perfect in carrying out your pre-defined pattern. At least, you give yourselves a chance to fight constructively. If you have mutually decided upon a pattern that fits your marriage, you will improve with time and practice.

Step Five: *Recognize the vulnerable feelings that lie beneath your anger.*

Imagine you are sitting in a park reading a book when someone comes up behind you with a knife and demands your valuables. How would you respond? You would not just sit there. Depending upon the situation you would either fight or flight. You would protect yourself as best you could. You would be angry.

Anger is a normal first response when we experience pain, whether emotional or physical. In the above example, you would probably have an underlying response of fear.

Anger is a way of protecting ourselves from pain and helps us feel we have retained a degree of control. This is especially true when it comes to emotional pain, where we often let ourselves feel vulnerable and weak. When we get angry, it gives us the sense of being in control when we feel out of control. Drawing upon our anger for protection and control is a major way we deal with the underlying emotional pain.

In chapter three, I shared the story of the intense anger I had towards Elaine when she would run late. The turning point for dealing with my anger in a healthy way was when the counselor helped me identify the vulnerable feeling behind my anger.

The counselor had to work with me for sometime before I was able to identify the feeling that was covered up with my anger. "How do you feel when Elaine is late?" asked the counselor. "I feel she doesn't care about my feelings and schedule." "How do you feel when you tell yourself she doesn't care about you?" "I feel lonely and unloved." I called upon my protection, my anger, to deal with the pain of feeling unloved and lonely.

When I was a boy, bad things happened when I came home late. I was punished, often severely. Being on time is ingrained into my psychic. Because bad things happened to me as a child, feeling scared and guilty correspond with being tardy. These vulnerable feelings carried over into my adult life. Now when Elaine is late I recognize the feelings that exist beneath my anger.

Elaine continues to be late. However, two positive things have happened as a result of identifying the feelings beneath my anger. First, her lateness has become less frequent. When I tried guilt and anger on Elaine, she seemed to get worse. Secondly, when she is late, rather than using anger to protect myself from the vulnerable feelings, I am able to call upon the intelligent part of me. She responds better and I feel better.

Step five requires being honest with yourself. It is not always easy to identify our vulnerable feelings and even more difficult to admit them to our spouse. Rarely am I able to identify the feeling beneath my anger at the moment I am feeling angry. But to do it minutes, hours or even days later is definitely an improvement in our fighting.

Go back to the last time you were angry at your spouse. Identify the vulnerable feeling beneath your anger, whether the feeling was inadequacy, rejection, disappointment or failure. Maybe you felt criticized by your spouse. What was the feeling? Take note of how you used anger to avoid the emotional pain that was taking place within you.

In the case of my wife's lateness, I needed some help from a counselor in order to identify the vulnerable feeling beneath my anger. You may need similar help. Actually, the vulnerable feeling can be a gift. Pain has a way of drawing attention to what needs attention in our life and relationships. We learn and grow through pain.

Step Six: *Give thanks for the commitment that is part of your married love.*

It is commitment that makes marriage a safe place to express differences and anger. Marriage commitment affords us the opportunity to come back to the conflicting issue once the anger has subsided. It is commitment that provides rational moments when we can discuss the issues as adult lovers rather than responding to each other like angry children.

Step Seven: *Here is a KISS that will be helpful for developing constructive patterns of anger.*

Both of you write down areas of conflict, general and specific. List the areas that are both major and minor issues. Now, as a couple, combine your list even if you do not agree with an issue on your spouse's list.

Using the numbers listed below, place a one, two, three, etc. beside each issue on your list. You may put several numbers beside a particular issue. This will provide food for creative and healthy communication about fighting and expression of anger:

1. I/we tend to avoid this issue.
2. This issue is not solvable.
3. This issue pertains to the reasons we got married. It may have to do with the fact you married an opposite.
4. This issue is too touchy. We need counseling.
5. This issue is solvable if . . .
6. This issue is my issue and not yours.
7. This issue is a life and death issue, i.e. top priority.
8. This issue arises out of my insecurity.
9. The cause is deeper than the presenting issue as stated. The underlying issue is . . .
10. I feel growth has been made on this issue.

Step Eight: *Communicate, Communicate, Communicate.*

Throughout your marriage, you will need to communicate continually about these steps for constructive fighting and anger. One step may work better than another, and this may change throughout the years.

Remember, the purpose of communication is not primarily to solve the issue you are fighting about. Some marriage experts say harmonious marriages have approximately ten irreconcilable differences. Realize that some marital issues may not be solvable.

Is it good to fight in front of the children? It depends on several things: the issue, the intensity of the anger and your decision as a couple. Personally, I think it is healthy to model for children that parents fight and get angry and still love each other. This is especially true when you share with them these steps you are seeking to apply to your conflicts. Most children, at some level, can understand the nature of the steps mentioned in this chapter. An open and honest discussion with your children about anger and how to deal with it will be a valuable model for your children, both now and later in life when they are in a committed relationship.

When our children were grade school age, Elaine and I were in the process of learning how to have a good fight. We shared openly with our children that we sometimes get angry at each other and then shared how we wanted to "do" our anger pattern. Although, at that age, they might not have fully understood; nevertheless it had a positive effect on how they felt when they saw us get angry.

One evening at the dinner table Elaine and I got into an argument in front of the kids. Rather than being frightened, they began to root for one of us. "Good job, Dad. You really got her on that one." "Go, Mom. You really nailed him." Elaine and I began to laugh.

This incident reassured us that sharing with them our anger pattern was a positive step and modeled for them what loving couples do.

I just finished reading this chapter for the eighth time. I had to admit to myself that Elaine and I must depend upon continued growth in the area of our anger patterns. Things are much different for us at age 72 than at 62 and 42. When you and your spouse address the issue of anger and fighting, remain open to how your feelings and pattern may change. They will be affected by multiple factors, such as age, children, job situation, health, finances, etc.

QUESTIONS FOR PERSONAL REFLECTION AND DISCUSSION WITH YOUR SPOUSE

KISS 1: What do you consider abnormal ways of fighting and expressing anger?

KISS 2: When it comes to being angry, what do you consider to be unrealistic expectations?

KISS 3: Why do you agree or disagree that working for resolution in a fight holds little value?

KISS 4: Share your response to using the word *angry* and *mad* rather than substituting another word. What is the effect of saying out loud, "I am angry at you?"

KISS 5: Say to your spouse, "You make me angry." Now, insert the words "choose" or "decide". "I am deciding to be angry at you." Share your response to the change of wording and to the idea that no one can make your feel something.

KISS 6: Recall a time when you were angry with your spouse. What was the vulnerable feeling that was beneath the anger?

7

The Ten Commandments For Making Love

Until my wedding night, I was a virgin. I thought I knew my way around the bedroom, but was I wrong. I soon realized that the junior high assemblies where we were "taught" about the birds and bees via a film omitted some pertinent information.

Once a year, we had what the students referred to as the "sex" assembly. We would gather in the auditorium and watch a film explaining the physiological aspects of sex. We would nervously laugh. Trying to be macho, the boys would let it be known they already knew that stuff.

Both Elaine and I were ignorant about matters of what makes healthy sexual relations. What we knew about sex was about 10% of what we should have known. We did not have a clue about the psychological and emotional aspects of sexuality.

My parents never brought up the issue of sex to me nor did they give me a book. So, when we were married, I was desperately in need of more knowledge than I found in my college anatomy book.

I had hoped the pastor would explain more about sex in our premarital counseling sessions, but he never mentioned it. I then went to the doctor for my annual physical and asked him for more information about sex. He was obviously uneasy and left the room as quickly as possible. My last hope was the church. I was sure I could get good sexual information there. I struck out for a third time. I, therefore, entered marriage as not only a physical virgin but also an informational virgin.

Now that I am the one in the premarital counseling chair, I make sure to cover the topic of sex and marriage. Our society may be bombarded with sexual imagery and the majority of couples may have already experienced sex, but I have found that whether a person has had sex before marriage has little to do with having healthy information about sex.

In fact, sexual difficulties in a marriage are the norm rather than the exception. This goes back to the fact that most of us were never given good information about the emotional dimension of sex. How our sex organs function and the emotions involved are a multifaceted and complex part of who we are. Layers of emotion and experience accompany the sexual part of a marital relationship.

I do not for one moment think I can cover this topic to the degree couples need. My goal is for the information in this chapter to generate positive dialogue and to motivate you, as a couple, to further investigate all aspects of sex.

There are no simple answers when it comes to sexual satisfaction in a marriage. What makes sense and works for one person/couple may be different from another person/couple. Because relationships are constantly evolving, discussing your feelings towards sex is essential throughout the life of your marriage.

Elaine and I have found the following ten commandments of lovemaking to be invaluable:

I have intentionally avoided using words such as, "most couples" or "most men/women" or "normally" or "usually". When it comes to the sexual part of marriage, what some might consider "normal" may or may not fit for you or your marriage. The ten commandments are not intended to provide a prescription, but rather an invitation into a process of continued dialogue and learning.

First Commandment: You shall build a healthy marriage because it is the prerequisite for healthy lovemaking.

Do you want to improve your lovemaking? The first way is to address the many issues that make up the dynamic of your marriage. The second way is to address the various emotional and physical issues that surround human sexuality. Most sexual problems have their roots in the emotional barriers we place between ourselves and our partner. Look at what is happening in your relationship before you look to what is happening in your sex life.

Lovemaking is a reflection and extension of marital interaction. When there are unresolved issues in a marriage they will show up in your lovemaking. Lovemaking is a stage for a drama where the dynamics of your marriage are acted out. You and your spouse are the leading actors in the drama. Building a healthy marriage produces a sexual drama that is filled with meaning. You will leave the auditorium where the drama took place and say, "Now that was an enjoyable performance." It was good because you had put a lot of time and thought into your marriage.

Second Commandment: You shall know that sex is a sacred gift from God.

The Bible is clear; our bodies are a gift from God. In Genesis, we are reminded that God looked at everything and said it was very good. (Genesis 1:31) In the New Testament, we are told to view our body as a "temple of the Holy Spirit within you, which you have from God . . . so glorify God in your body." (First Corinthians 6:19) In Romans 12:1, we read, "I appeal to you, by the mercies of God, to present your bodies as a living sacrifice, holy and acceptable to God."

Approaching lovemaking as a sacred gift from God places sex where it belongs and was intended—in the context of a committed love relationship.

Many names have been used to speak of God. Some have referred to God as "Life Force" or "Field of Energy." Sex is one of the many ways this field of energy runs through our bodies in an expression of God's love. This life force creates new life. Those who receive sex as God's gift focus on increasing God's love rather than increasing their sex drive. Sex will be transformed from a way of gratifying ourselves to a way of expressing our gratitude to God. Making love will be filled with God's purpose and not simply a way to be pleasured.

God's grace and unconditional love are especially important in light of the fact that a great amount of fear and guilt surround issues of sexuality. Creativity, pleasure and freedom have been stifled by messages telling us sex is naughty, sinful and secretive. God's unconditional love frees us to enter into lovemaking as recreation and re-creation, both part of God's gift.

This grace gives us permission to be patient with ourselves and our spouses. Fulfilling lovemaking calls for trial and error. God's grace and forgiveness affords couples the freedom to learn with and from each other without blame, guilt, fear or hesitation.

Those who adhere to this second commandment live each day with gratitude. Grateful people do not allow past mistakes or errors to get in the way of doing what is needed to cultivate a fulfilling sex life.

When my boys were teenagers, the United Methodist Church offered sexuality seminars for teens. Not only were they giving proper information about sex, but they were also showing the teenagers it was OK to talk about such things in the church. This was one way to let our teens know sex is sacred and God's gift.

Some people are alarmed by what has been termed the "sexual revolution." Is there too much openness about sex? Is there too much promiscuity? Is there too much skin exposed in magazines, videos and TV? Regardless of how you answer these questions, I doubt seriously whether there is any turning back.

The only solution is to flood the issues and discussions of sexuality with the truth that sex is God's sacred gift. This would help us as a society to focus on the redemptive aspects of sexuality. This truth will ensure that sex is not misused and abused, but remains a healthy, beautiful and sacred part of our society and our marriages.

Prior to viewing our lovemaking as a gift from God, Elaine and I did a poor job of communicating about our emotional and physical differences. We avoided certain aspects of our sexual relationship. Fear and guilt were contaminating our lovemaking. Receiving our sexuality as God's gift freed us to increase communication about our lovemaking. For example, we were freed to express openly and honestly our wants and desires. The new found freedom did not eliminate all the barriers. The open communication did set us on a new path that has proven invaluable over the years

Accepting the truth that our life and sexuality are gifts from God enables us to affirm only God makes love. Rather than telling your spouse you want to make love, think about replacing "make" with other words that reflect an understanding that it is God who makes love. "Honey, tonight let's build, express, fashion, create, shape our love."

Third Commandment: You shall understand how lovemaking is influenced by the childhood messages about sexuality you did or did not receive.

For a number of reasons, many of us grew up feeling sex was dirty and naughty. While it is normal for certain aspects of sex to remain personal and private, not getting any information about sex as a child can lead to misunderstanding about sex.

For instance, many of us grew up thinking there was something wrong with masturbation or wet dreams. Why? Was it because discussions about normal bodily functions were off limits in many families? For me, the nonverbal message I received was that sexual feelings were wrong.

When I was a senior in high school, I walked into the kitchen and saw my father pinch my mother's backend. I was beyond shocked. But I was more shocked that I was shocked. Why did a normal marriage flirtation shock a high school senior?

Fast forward 15 or so years when my father died. Within three years of his death, my mother, who was in her late 50s, fell in love and remarried. I asked her why she was remarrying. She shared several reasons, but the one that shocked me: she missed having sex. Why would such a statement from my mother shock a middle-aged married man?

Being shocked had to do with the fact that sex was not openly discussed in my home. For me, sex was associated with guilt and shame. Certainly sex was not something that should be fun and enjoyed. Sex was associated with dos and don'ts rather than with how sex is a sacred gift from God.

When I was six years old, my father walked into my room where I playing doctor with my buddy. I had my clothes off and my friend was examining me. My father said, "Put on your clothes and come downstairs." I knew I was in for big trouble. When my friend and I walked into the kitchen, my father said, "Go outside and play." The incident was never mentioned again. Do you think this incident had a positive or negative affect on the attitude I have about sexuality and took into my marriage? This is one of the few times in my upbringing that I received a positive message about sex. The way my father handled the situation communicated to me that sex and curiosity about sex are normal.

If your lovemaking is not completely satisfying, go back and think about the many messages you received as a child and teenager about sex. What was said or not said about sex in your home? What did you see or not see growing up that shaped your ideas and attitude toward sexuality? Make note of the positive and helpful messages as well as the negative and unhelpful ones. In what way do the messages play out in your lovemaking?

Fourth Commandment: You shall take the initiative in letting your spouse know when and how you want to make love.

Who initiates the lovemaking in your marriage? Does one spouse initiate more than another? When you tell your spouse you want to make love, is it direct and verbal; or do you expect your partner to pick up on your subtle expression of desire? Do you keep score as to how many times you asked first?

Reflect on the following15 scenarios associated to those times when a spouse initiates or refrains from initiating lovemaking. You may add others:

1. One partner initiates lovemaking and the other is grateful and responsive.
2. One spouse initiates and the other says, "Yes" even though he/she is not in the mood. In this scenario the sexual encounter may or may not turn out to be satisfying.
3. One partner initiates, but feels the spouse's positive response is because he/she is being asked and not a honest desire.
4. One partner initiates and the spouse's "no", is followed with "later when I . . ." A valid reason is given and the reason is received with understanding.
5. One partner initiates and receives a "no", followed by an excuse that is not the real reason.
6. One spouse initiates and hears, "I'm not in the mood." This is said in such a loving and reassuring way that he/she does not feel rejected.
7. Even when a spouse says in a loving way that he/she is not in the mood, the partner chooses to feel rejected.
8. One spouse initiates and keeps score on how many times he/she has been turned down. The initiator will says such things as, "I asked you first four times. I'm not going to ask again until you ask me first." Rather than considering that the refusal was loving and valid, the scorekeeper feels one refusal deserves another. Whenever a spouse initiates lovemaking the wife/husband may put a parent face on their spouse. No one wants to sleep with a parent. In our home, as we were growing up, our parents were the ones who initiated when and if an event was to take place. As children we did what was asked. Often these same feelings will surface when love making is initiated by your spouse.
9. When there has been conflict and anger, you can expect it to affect the initiation issue.
10. Some are reluctant to initiate lovemaking because they think it is being selfish. Consequently, they feel guilty. Guilt is a major obstacle to healthy lovemaking. Ask yourself whether letting your spouse know your desires and wants is selfish or is simply being honest and direct.

Personally, I have a sense of relief when my wife declares what she wants. As we learned in one of our marriage seminars, each person is responsible for their own orgasm. This is in contrast to thinking we are responsible for our spouse's pleasure. This means being open and honest about what we want and when we want it. This includes allowing our spouse the freedom to respond yes, no, maybe or let me think about it. It is an expression of love when we are open and vulnerable with our spouse about our desires. This makes both partners mutually giving and responsible.

11. Who initiates love making is affected by role expectations. For example, some couples succumb to the dangers of stereotyping the man as the pursuer and the women as the one to be pursued. Women may feel expressing their desire is a turn off. They do not want to be perceived as aggressive, needy or selfish. Men may not express their wants because of being perceived as weak, dominating, demanding or selfish. When one or both partners choose to refrain from expressing their sexual wants directly and openly, feelings are often suppressed. Those feelings come out later, often in unhelpful and unhealthy ways.

12. Who initiates lovingmaking is affected by how a person feels about his/her body. Those who do not feel good about their external appearance will be slow to initiate lovemaking. Do you feel your body is attractive? If the answer is no, sometimes, rarely, or not sure, you may not be forthright and direct when it comes to initiating lovemaking.

We let society and others define what is attractive. It is usually connected to body size or shape. Since we are all aging, how ridiculous is it to allow someone else to define whether or not we have an attractive body? Again, the importance of self-esteem emerges. When we feel attractive on the inside, we will feel attractive enough on the outside. External appearance will be much less of a factor when it comes to initiating lovemaking.

13. Don't expect your spouse to read your mind. It is best to be direct and honest. Your spouse may or may not choose to give what you request; but, at least the lines of communication are open and clear. Your spouse may or may not be able to pick up on non-verbal hints.

14. Along with being assertive by initiating *when* we want to make love is sharing *how* we want or don't want to make love. This may include such things as place, variety, attire, position or time of day. Again there are risks involved here. What if our partner does not want what we want? At least, the lines of communication are open.

Throughout your marriage, you should expect changes when it comes to initiating sex. Different stages in life and factors such as life circumstances, stress, work, aging, marital conflict, self-esteem and psychological history all affect the initiation issue.

Fifth Commandment: You shall talk about how frequently you want to make love.

Several years ago a friend asked me how often my wife and I make love. I was fairly sure I knew why he was asking the question. After talking with him, I discovered I was right. He wanted to know what was normal.

I continued by asking him questions about his marriage. I am always suspicious when I get a question like this one. There is usually something going on in the marriage that needs to be addressed before dealing with the issue of frequency. We talked for awhile about the underlying issue he and his wife were facing, or in this case, not facing.

I then turned to the issue of what is normal. I shared with him that there is no such thing as normal when it comes to how frequently couples make love. What is normal for one couple may not be normal for another couple.

Your "normal" will be decided by a number of issues, such as the following:

1. Frequency depends upon a person's age, although some couples in their sixties have told me they make love more often than they did in their thirties. Older couples have had years of working through their sexual issues and may not have the degree of performance anxiety of younger couples. Performance anxiety is a factor when it comes to deciding how frequently a couple wants to make love.
2. One partner may deal with stress differently which can affect how often he/she wants to make love.
3. Low sexual desire in one or both partners is a common problem in many marriages. Frequency is affected by low sexual desire. This may be the result of physical factors, such as the effects of prescription and/or recreational drugs. Tranquilizers, antihistamines, nicotine and

alcohol are examples that may affect sexual appetite. Certain medical conditions can also influence sexual desire. A check-up with your doctor can determine if there is a physical problem causing low sexual desire. Of course, the low sexual desire may be related to how a couple is or is not dealing with the central issues in their marriage.

4. Frequency may have to do with energy. Some partners simply are made up differently in terms of energy level.

5. There are a variety of emotional issues connected to the frequency of making love. Many of the issues can be traced to our psychological history, such as being in control and being close. Basic differences between males and females can be a factor.

6. The issue of frequency is complicated by the reality that each of us changes over the course of a marriage. The change is slow and often unnoticed.

When it comes to how often you and your spouse make love, what other factors would you add to this list? Which of these six issues are relevant to your marriage? The fact that you and your spouse are different when it comes to the frequency issue does not guarantee there is a problem. It is normal for couples to have different wants and needs. If the issue of frequency is not talked about on a regular basis, hurt and tension are sure to follow.

A sex therapist and author had just ended a lecture on sex in marriage. A man approached the "expert" and said, "I appreciate what you said in your talk. I especially liked the part having to do with the frequency issues. We have sex once a year." The lecturer thought the man's response was somewhat unusual and so he asked, "How do you feel about that?" The man smiled as he said, "Oh, I feel fine." "You seem to be OK with having sex once a year. You even appear happy. Why is that?" "Because," said the man, "tonight's the night."

Sixth Commandment: You shall address openly and directly the issues of timing.

When the timing issues are not addressed frustration and hurt feelings usually follow.

Timing has to do with who has an orgasm first and who goes second. Some couples have decided they want to have simultaneous orgasms. I know of couples who have decided the husband goes first, and I know of couples who have decided the wife goes first. Some couples feel if both climax at the same time, they do not fully enjoy their partner's satisfaction because they are so caught up in their own. Of course, there is no right or wrong here.

Studies report 20-30 percent of couples climax at the same time. Some sex therapists think even these percentages are too high. Frustration often happens when couples are trying to have simultaneous orgasms. Typically in a given sexual encounter, the male has one orgasm. Female orgasm is more complex and variable. A woman might be nonorgasmic, singly orgasmic, or multiorgasmic, either during foreplay, intercourse or afterplay.

This raises the question about orgasm being the goal of lovemaking. For some making love is like running a race. The goal is to get to the finish line as quickly as possible. Couples may want to consider lovemaking more like a leisurely jog through the woods or on the beach. The goal is to enjoy the run/walk without being preoccupied with a finish line. Take time to enjoy the journey. This may be as important, or more important, than the destination.

Some have used the analogy of a ladder when talking about sex. When someone thinks the most important purpose of a ladder (lovemaking) is to reach the top (climax), unnecessary pressure, frustration and hurt occur. When we take time, maybe even pause on each rung of the ladder and experience satisfaction from the process of climbing, any potential pressures that might take place in lovemaking are minimized. The climb itself is as much part of the goal as reaching the top.

Much sexual dysfunction comes from the pressure of reaching a climax and/or climaxing at the same time. For men, the pressure can result in premature ejaculation, loss of erection or impotence. For women, the pressure can result in failure to climax by thinking she is taking too long or that her partner thinks she is taking too long. When orgasm is not the only goal, intimacy, closeness and love will override pressure to perform.

This insight is emphasized by Barbara DeAngelis in her book, *How to Make Love All the Time*. She talks of having "greedy sex or gourmet sex." She writes; "Imagine your body as a big container of energy. When you start to have sex, you feel an increase in the energy inside your body, starting in your genitals. As the energy starts to build, you make a choice: You may focus your energy on your genitals for maximum pleasure, or spread out the energy all over the body, especially into the area of the emotions."

For most people, sex consists of making the first choice—trying to stuff as much pleasure and energy into the genitals as quickly as possible. I call this greedy sex. Learning to have gourmet sex means taking the time to integrate the sexual energy throughout the body so you can experience even more energy, resulting in more vitality, more joy—more love.

Timing issues are complicated by the inconvenient gender gap. When it comes to arousal and climax, men are faster up and faster down. This may be a generalization, but it seems to be the case for most men. Women tend to be slower up and slower down. Further complications happen because this general difference between male and female may change throughout the course of the marriage, depending on many factors.

Another factor related to the timing issue is the time of day lovemaking takes place. Again, the husband and wife may or may not be on the same page. For example, in my marriage Elaine is a night person. Her energy level is highest at night. My highest energy is in the morning. Men's testosterone, a primary hormone responsible for sexual desire, peaks at seven or eight in the morning.

As I have grown older, my energy level is very low after dark. My wife is more turned on when it is dark than in the daylight. This may not be your situation. I only share our experience as a way of pointing out how this aspect of timing is an issue to be addressed together, especially because we will probably change throughout the course of our married life.

Seventh Commandment: You shall be creative and free in your lovemaking.

"I am not sure what is happening," a man reported to me. "When it comes to sex it seems as if the chemistry is gone. I still love my wife, but I don't feel the sexual excitement and magic we used to have. I guess the old saying is true: familiarity breeds contempt."

Do you agree? Does familiarity breed contempt? Does sameness lead to sexual indifference? The answer is, it depends. It depends upon a choice each partner makes. Remember, no one can make you feel something. We choose how we are going to respond in a situation, including making love to the same person for a lifetime. It can be an uninspiring routine or it can be exciting, exhilarating and electrifying. That is always your decision.

The decision to insure lovemaking is stimulating and invigorating will happen when we are free and creative.

Commandment number one reminds us that being sexually free comes primarily from accepting the truth that sex is God's gift. Accepting this truth about the nature and activity of God generates a grateful and humble spirit. When people are filled with gratitude and humility, astonishing and creative things happen in life, including in our lovemaking. Such a spirit turns into freedom which is successfully converted into creativity.

Sometimes people become inhibited, self-conscious and locked into routine. When we are sexually free, our creative juices take over and our imaginations run wild. I suggest the following ideas for being free and creative in making love:

First, make sure to keep romance in your relationship. I know many couples who do this by setting aside a date night. The date may or may not include sex. The date definitely includes romance. If you forgot how to be romantic, think back and do the things you did while you were dating. Remember the little things you did to win his/her love, how you constantly tried to please. Sometimes we get married and the chase is off. Why? Part of the excitement of our courting days was the chase, including the sneaking around. Now that's a creative idea for being romantic.

Second, be creative as you think of places to make love other than the bedroom. Many couples report their best sex happens some place other than the house. The house is a turnoff for some. It is where we have responsibility, pay bills, argue, respond to children, etc . . .

Remember the backseat of the car or the hidden place in the woods? I could suggest many creative ideas for places and ways to make love. You will think of them all, and more, when you free up your creative spirit. There are many resources that can assist your creativity. One is *How To Make Love To The Same Person For The Rest Of Your Life,* by Dagmar O'Connor.

When it comes to being creative in making love, many couples crave variety. Creatively exploring unfamiliar and unusual places, positions and attire can increase sexual fulfillment. And remember, deviant and perverted sex is what two people do and only one person enjoys it.

There is a free/fun child within each of us. The child part of us is where our creativity exists. Note the key part of the word, fore*play.* Our playful child often gets squelched in our approach to lovemaking.

Many couples report they are too busy to make love; have sex, yes, but not make love. Consequently, many don't relax and/or don't know how to relax. Relaxation is an important part of being creative. I know I do my best creative thinking when I am relaxed, even if the relaxation is through exercising. Many couples report having their best sex when they are on vacation. That is a time when their free child is most active.

Recall the feelings of excitement and satisfaction when you get something new, such as new shoes, car, house, or an outfit. You feel like a little child. Or recall the excitement and satisfaction when the relationship with your spouse was new. There is something about "new" that is appealing. Lovemaking can be new as we apply our creativity. You do not need or want a new pair of shoes or a new car if the one you have is new. Likewise we do not need or want a new relationship if we are creatively applying newness to our lovemaking.

Your creativity will also distinguish the difference between new and different. Your lovemaking may or may not need to be different. Novelty and new are not necessary for an exciting sex life. There is nothing wrong with making love in familiar ways. Indeed, a lot can be said for the feeling of security that goes along with the familiar. The familiar and same can be experienced as new when our free child and creativity are at work.

A common way for couples to express their creativity and fun child is through the world of fantasy. Don't make fantasizing part of your creative expression in making love if it does not fit under what you consider normal and acceptable. Many of us have thoughts in the privacy of our minds that we tell ourselves are wrong. Part of the appeal of fantasizing is the freedom to incorporate into lovemaking things that are risky, forbidden, illicit, mischievous and naughty. Many unnecessarily expend energy doing what is nearly impossible, i.e. getting rid of those thoughts. It is difficult to get rid of normal thoughts and feelings. Fantasy is a healthy and creative way to use those thoughts and feelings to improve married love.

I remember when I had hepatitis. The doctor told me the one thing I could not have was cantaloupe. Yes, cantaloupe was the one thing I craved. Fantasy allows us to have what we cannot have and saves us from doing stupid things, such as having an affair.

Some think fantasies of having an affair is a symptom of an unhappy marriage. Others have increased the joy of their lovemaking by having an affair with their own husband/wife. What keeps someone from infidelity is not lack of fantasy or desire. Intelligence, commitment and knowledge of the long range consequences are more influential in remaining faithful than fantasizing about having an affair. Fantasy makes more sense than the lasting hurt of an actual affair.

Therefore, plan to have an affair with your spouse. Depending on which source you hear, the percent of married persons who have affairs is higher than any of us believe is healthy. Being incensed about the evils of an affair is unlikely to reduce the number taking place. What will reduce the number is the freedom and creativity that goes along with having affairs with your wife/husband. In this scenario, no one has cheated. You are playing a game together. You mutually decide upon the rules of this affair/game. There is no winner or loser. Both are winners.

Is fantasy a crutch? If you think it is, don't do it. If it is a way to express your creativity and increase your married love, go for it. Experiment with it. For example, because most of us do not have a body that is a ten, fantasize your body (or your spouse's body) being as fit and shapely as the most attractive movie star. It would also be helpful to differentiate between thinking a fantasy and physically acting out a fantasy. You may or may not want to do both.

Your creativity will grow and flourish when you intentionally plan and schedule lovemaking. This may include rethinking the idea that intentionally planning sex makes it something other than spontaneous. When I suggested to one couple that they be intentional about planning when and how they make love, they responded, "That makes it all so contrived and artificial. Sex is supposed to come naturally." What keeps you from intentionally creating relaxed and inviting circumstances where spontaneity can happen? If your spontaneous lovemaking is working for you, be happy. However, spontaneous lovemaking often regresses into routine and habit. There is no better way to be spontaneous than using your creativity to intentionally plan spontaneity.

Intentionally planning lovemaking presents an opportunity to be sensitive to each other's feelings, schedule and energy level. Planning lovemaking insures that good communication is taking place rather than assuming you know when your partner might be in the mood. Scheduling lovemaking allows you to take full advantage of your creativity.

We all know the benefits of planning our day or a vacation. The planning is important so we can get done what we want to get done. We can take into account everything that might be an obstacle to accomplishing what we want to get done. The kind of lovemaking that confronts obstacles and gets done what we want is more likely to happen when we intentionally plan ahead. The planning comes under the category of foreplay. It may even include an obscene phone call to your spouse during the day. Anticipation is a great trigger.

When your creativity is directed towards lovemaking, you have the best of both worlds. You have the trust and security of a committed relationship. At the same time you have the thrill and excitement of adventure and novelty. Making love to the same person the rest of our life becomes an experience that never grows old.

Eighth Commandment: You shall constantly seek to be informed on the many issues surrounding human sexuality.

This information will come through both your own experience and the knowledge that is available from professionals in the area of human sexuality.

It is normal to have a degree of difficulty in the sexual dimension of our marriage. One marriage therapist even goes so far as to use the words "mismatched" and "incompatible" when referring to what most couples experience sexually. This does not mean we are stupid about matters of sex, but it does point to the importance of this commandment.

Some people never learn essential sex information because they are too embarrassed to admit they have questions, let alone openly ask their questions. Being informed may mean unlearning some misinformation we accumulated over the years.

Almost every marriage book devotes one chapter to the sexual aspect of marriage. The Internet has a wealth of information about human sexuality. Some of the material is helpful and informative. Some, in my judgment, is questionable and distasteful. On your search engine, type in "marriage" or "human sexuality". At one point, I typed in "embarrassing sexual questions" and uncovered many good articles. Narrowing your search will bring forth information about the biological, psychological, medical, emotional and spiritual aspects of human sexuality.

Some of the best information will come from your own sexual experiences as a couple. This information will come through trial and error as well as your successes. Refrain from being critical of yourself or your partner. Learn and grow from your many experiences of making love.

Ninth Commandment: You shall recognize and acknowledge how your insecurities affect your lovemaking.

In chapter two, I noted how our insecurities are manifested in every aspect of marriage, but none as prevailing as the sexual aspect.

It would be helpful for couples to ask themselves how their insecurities play out in the issues related to lovemaking. For example, ask yourself how low sexual desire and feelings of rejection are tied to low self-esteem? How do your insecurities have a direct and powerful impact on the issues of frequency, timing, initiative and conflict? Low self-esteem will not allow a person to say clearly, "I want" when it comes to issues surrounding frequency and style. Dissatisfaction with any of these issues is grounded in dissatisfaction with oneself.

The more secure we feel by loving ourselves as one of God's special gifts, the better we will be able to deal lovingly and creatively with the complexities of human sexuality.

Tenth Commandment: You shall communicate, communicate, communicate.

All of the previous nine commandments cry out for continual communication. Problems are likely to develop if couples do not keep the lines open.

With the inevitable changes that surround making love to the same person for a lifetime, continual communication must be a priority.

In chapter nine, we will look at ways to commit yourself to communicating openly and honestly about your relationship.

QUESTIONS FOR PERSONAL REFLECTION
AND
DISCUSSION WITH YOUR SPOUSE

KISS 1: On a scale of one to ten evaluate your degree of knowledge about the issues surrounding lovemaking, both when you got married and at the present time.

KISS 2: Which of the 15 issues related to taking the initiative pertain most to your marriage?

KISS 3: Discuss how and why you are different (or similar) when it comes to asking for what you want and taking the initiative. What percent of the time do you think or feel you initiate sex and what percent of the time do you perceive your spouse initiates?

KISS 4: How do you feel about the frequency of your lovemaking? What are the major factors that affect how frequently you desire sex? What is the best way to satisfy your different desires?

KISS 5: What aspects of the timing issue would you like to discuss with your partner? Share with your partner how you feel about the ladder/race/gourmet illustration.

KISS 6: Each partner list ways for keeping your lovemaking creative and free.

KISS 7: Share your thoughts and feelings about intentionally planning and scheduling a time to make love.

KISS 8: Share with your partner how your insecurities are expressed in your lovemaking.

KISS 9: On a scale of one to ten, how do you evaluate the effectiveness of your and your partner's communication about lovemaking? Why are you or are you not hesitant in communicating about the various issues of this chapter? Which of the issues do you find are more difficult to discuss?

8

How Our Differences Turn Us On and Off

Think back to when you were dating your spouse. What three personality traits attracted you to each other? Be specific. Refrain from putting love and looks on your list. What is it that led you to say, "I want to spend the rest of my life with this person?"

Now look over your list and ask yourself this question: "Are these personality characteristics a source of tension in my marriage?"

It's true, what initially attracts us to a person often becomes a source of tension in the marriage. In fact, throughout our marriage what attracts us to our spouse continue to both turn us on and turn us off.

When Elaine and I were courting, I was attracted to her vivacious and outgoing mannerism. I still love her energy and enthusiasm; at the same time, these personality traits are a continual source of tension in our marriage. Elaine was attracted to me because of my tendency to be reflective and introspective. She still likes these qualities, but at times they drive her crazy and produce tension in our relationship.

We are subconsciously drawn to someone who has personality characteristics we do not possess. For instance, I needed someone to spice up my life. I told myself she would be the excitement I needed. I had concluded my life would not be so monotonous with her energy and enthusiasm. On the other hand, Elaine needed someone who would level her out. I would help her to not be so scattered. Elaine prefers lots of activity. My brother calls her "Little Ms. Commotion." On the weekend she prefers to be with friends. I prefer some activity, but not commotion. I would prefer to spend the weekend with just the two of us.

Our opposite personality traits complemented each other, but it was only after some years of marriage that we uncovered how our opposite personality traits were putting a stress on our relationship.

I recall years ago when we went to see a counselor. I don't remember the specific problem, but we knew we needed some help. After listening to us for awhile, the counselor pointed out how different we were. Initially we both were defensive. We pointed how we like the same things: sports, family time, traveling, playing cards, religion and politics. How can you say we are different? It was a major turn around in our relationship when Elaine and I realized we were, in many ways, opposites. We began to understand how our differences were causing tension even though we still liked the particular character trait of each other.

Remember when you announced to your friends that you were getting married? You probably told your friends and family that you found someone who is "interesting." This meant we found someone who had qualities we did not have. We seek to marry someone who complements our weaknesses and compensates for our deficiencies. We feel connected to a part of us we either lost or never fully developed.

For example, if I feel insecure about my ability to relate to others, I look for someone who is outgoing and personable. If I feel insecure about expressing my feelings, I tell myself I can find security in marrying someone who openly expresses feelings. If I tend to be a risk taker, I get security from someone who is organized and is a planner. This is a way we can feel more secure amidst our insecurity.

Here's what it boils down to: **we marry a person who has at least one or two personality characteristics that are the opposite of ours. Initially, we may see the characteristic as something we like; but often what**

originally attracted us to our spouse becomes a source of tension. At the same time, we probably continue to like the opposite personality trait.

Elaine is an extrovert and I am an introvert. This does not mean I don't like to be around people and she does. Most extroverts appreciate time when they can be alone, and most introverts enjoy being with people. It is a matter of where a person gets his/her energy. Extroverts are energized by being around people. An introvert gets energy by spending time alone.

Elaine and I have dealt with this dynamic in several ways. Sometimes we compromise. Sometimes I will attend a social event with her even if I prefer to stay at home. Sometimes she attends the social event by herself. Prior to our awareness of how we were opposites, she would attend an event by herself and resent it. I would go to the event and let my resentment be known in obnoxious ways. Realizing opposites attract has freed each of us to allow the other to be who they are, rather than expecting them to change and be what we want them to be.

When counseling married couples, I am fascinated by how often problems stem from the fact they are opposites. I usually begin by asking them to share why they have come for counseling. Nine times out of ten each spouse will begin telling me what their spouse is doing or saying that is irritating them. The focus is on what their spouse is doing and saying that is different (opposite) from how they think things should be done.

The dynamics of opposites attracting seems to be a natural part of life (and marriage.) This can be seen in one branch of physics called magnetism. Magnetism deals with magnets and magnetic properties. A magnet is made up of a north and south pole. The poles on the opposite ends of a magnet act differently toward each other. If the north pole of one magnet comes close to the north pole of another magnet, the two poles repel (push away from) each other. Two south poles also repel each other. But a north and a south pole attract each other and stick together. Two poles that are the same repel each other. Two poles that are different attract each other.

It is interesting how this law of physics plays out in a marriage. Often the gap in the marriage relationship is bridged by opposite personality characteristics while personality traits that are alike tend to repel.

Awareness of this dynamic enables married couples to begin dealing with the complexities of personalities. An atmosphere of learning and growth comes by acknowledging how the dynamic of marrying an opposite works. One couple in a premarital counseling session said to me, "We were attracted to each other like magnets." Initially, they saw a particular trait as something they liked. Seldom do newlyweds understand how the same personality traits can become a source of tension.

The premise that opposites attract can be a valuable resource for your process of self-examination. You may be an exception to the law of opposites, but I have yet to meet a couple for whom this premise is not relevant, at least to some degree. Therefore, I invite you to learn more about this common source of marital tension.

Below is a list of opposite personality characteristics that will assist you in evaluating how you and your spouse were initially attracted to each other. From this list, you may uncover many or only a few that apply to your relationship.

Take time and add to this list as it applies to your relationship. It should be obvious that each opposite is not mutually exclusive. For example, every spender has a part of them that is concerned about saving and vice versa. Every follower has a desire to lead, and every leader, at times, wants to follow. Nevertheless, most of us have a number of opposite personality patterns that are primary and preferred. Each opposite holds great potential for complementing our spouse.

Prefer sports	Prefer music, drama and art
Like activities that stimulate the mind	Like activities that stimulate the entire body
Have a strong work ethic; play later	Have a strong play ethic; enjoy now and finish work later

Derive satisfaction by completing a project	Derive satisfaction from the process of doing the task
Religion is important	Can take or leave religion
Facts and logic are important	Common sense, imagination and innovation are important
Leader	Follower
Organization and structure are needed	Flexibility and ability to adapt are needed
Make decisions quickly and easily	Take time to think through consequences of a decision
Birthdays and holidays are important, including buying gifts	Special days and gifts are overrated
Adapts slowly to change	Adapts quickly to change
Use the head for determining practical results	Use the heart for understanding how people feel and interact
Gregarious and outgoing	Calm and quiet
Complete a task in a timely fashion	Procrastinate and keep options open
Tend to avoid conflict	Deal with conflict upfront

What people think is not important	Want to please others, if possible
Overextend; exceed your limits	Stay within what is possible
Suspicious and guarded	Trusting
Intellectualize	Emphasis on feelings
Bring up pertinent facts	Bring up new possibilities
Focus on what needs attention now	Focus on how the future would be affected
Time is important; punctual	Uncomfortable with tight schedules; frequently late
Prefer to plan ahead	Prefer to remain flexible
Want to follow rules	Want to adapt to each situation
A stickler for rules	Rules are to be interpreted
Respect and value tradition	Respect the new and experimental
Want structure and limits risks	Risk taker
Being assertive and decisive are valued	Having patience and thinking things through are valued

Foreplay consists of eating out and going to a movie (This takes five hours)	Foreplay consists of turning on the music and dimming the lights (This takes two minutes)
Material things are important	Material things are unimportant
It is important for people to do a job	The focus is on praising people for the job they do
Saver	Spender
Neatness is a good thing	Neatness is overrated
Prefer to deal immediately with problems and stress	Prefer to postpone dealing with problems and stress
Tend to see glass half full	Tend to see glass half empty
Marathoner (stay with something for a good length of time; leave money in stock market and trust long projections)	Sprinter (do a project and move on to next project; try to time stock market)
Introvert (You get energy from by being by yourself)	Extrovert (You get energy from being with people)
You think about sex frequently	You think about sex infrequently
A morning person	A night person

Another reality that needs to be added to the above list is the difference between males and females. We often speak of marrying someone of the "opposite" sex. Various authors have documented gender differences and at the same time caution us about making generalizations.

Walk up to a grade school playground and notice how the children voluntarily separate themselves by gender. The play activities of boys are more aggressive, usually accompanied by rough-and-tumble play and unrestrained movements. The girls' play is not as loud and requires less space to do their play activity.

There appears to be a biological difference between the opposite sexes. The physiological factors are amplified and crystallized by how our culture responds to innate gender differences. Can our spouse ever fully understand us, given the basic dissimilarities of men and women? When many of the differences stem from biological factors and are solidified by social forces that shape our personality, it is easy to see the challenges involved in married love.

A recent report by ABC News indicated increasing scientific research is telling us that in many ways men and women are genetically different, if not opposites. Recent reports show newborn males and females have different circuitry and hormones that dramatically shape their future thoughts, feelings and behavior in the first years of life.

These differences are explained in a book by Dr. LouAnn Brizendine, a neuropsychiatrist and author of *The Female Brain*. New brain imagining technology and sophisticated animal studies provide scientists with tools to map human emotions and gender differences. Due to this revolutionary technology, we now know that areas for emotional memory and communication are larger in the female brain. Perhaps this explains why, on the average, women remember fights men insist never happened and why women use 20,000 words a day, while men use only 7,000. In fact, neuro-imaging shows, early on, the typical teen girl has a stronger connection between the areas of the brain that control impulse (the amygdala) and judgment (the prefrontal cortex). When it comes to emotions, Dr. Brizendine says girls have their own area that is twice as large as boys—the hippocampus, which is the seat of emotional memory.

The female brain uses many centers in both hemispheres that activate in response to faces, voices and expressions. Men, however, use only one side of their brain. Dr. Brizendine insists that despite "hard wiring" of our brain chemistry, we do have free will. But the science is undeniable; powerful hormones and the complex circuitry of the brain do shape our behavior and, therefore, our destiny.

At the same time, some of the differences between men and women do not always hold true. John Gray sold a lot of books advocating the point of view that men and women are innately different. They even come from different planets. *MEN ARE FROM MARS, Women Are from Venus* is the title of his book. One of Gray's major points is that men go into their cave. He states when men are stressed they become increasingly focused and withdraw into the cave of their minds. Men draw upon the rational. Women focus on the emotions involved. Women desire to have the issues aired.

This is a generality that may hold true in most cases. But I know women who withdraw in the face of stress. Likewise, I know men who will not leave the scene, get emotional and prefer to talk it through at the moment. I know several couples where the wife is interested in sports and the stock market, while the husband has only a passing interest in these aspects of life. I know of men who are highly emotional while their wives guard their emotions. And more and more we are seeing stay-at-home husbands while the women are the "breadwinners." These realities do not alter the tendency to marry an opposite. It simply tells us to be cautious when making generalities about personality characteristics of the opposite sex.

Even the way our spouse says, "I love you," is often different, if not opposite. One author (Gary Chapman, *THE Five LOVE LANGUAGES*) suggests we must learn the preferred love language of our spouse in order to fully express our love for her/him. Chapman's five languages are: 1. Verbal expressions of affirmation, appreciation, encouragement 2. Quality time; giving undivided attention 3. Receiving gifts as symbols of love 4. Acts of service; doing something you know your spouse would like 5. Physical touch.

Chapman points out that while all five languages may communicate love, each of us has a primary language of love we prefer. For example, what if you are married to a person from France who speaks both French and English? You can talk in English but he/she may prefer French because that is their primary language. If you do not know French, obviously it would be helpful to your relationship if you spent some time learning your spouse's primary language. Therefore, if my preferred way to express love for my wife is giving her gifts but she prefers verbal expressions of appreciation, it would be helpful if I spent time learning to speak her preferred language of love.

The other day my wife told me when I leave the toilet seat up she feels I don't care. Putting the seat down communicates the fourth language of love. She feels I care. If putting the toilet seat down says to her, "I love you," the seat will go down. I can learn to speak her language of love. Likewise, my wife could verbalize all day that she loves and appreciates me (language number one). But the words do not communicate her love as much as when she says nothing and rubs my head at night before we go to sleep (language four and five).

Seldom do individuals prefer the same language of love. We become confused when our spouse does not respond in the way we want and expect. It is important to identify and speak your spouse's primary love language, which more than likely is the opposite or, at least, different from yours. In the beginning we were attracted to our spouse because she/he spoke a language of love that was different. We may have been fascinated by that language. Part of us may have liked the sound of our spouse's love language. Later in the marriage, we began to prefer our own love language and wish our spouse would use it when communicating love.

Sometimes birth order illustrates how opposite attracts. Notice the personality characteristics of oldest, youngest, only and middle children. Check and see if you married an opposite.

In my marriage, an oldest married a youngest. At the time, we did not understand that subconsciously we were choosing an opposite. We have struggled with the issues that have arisen from an oldest marrying a youngest. It was helpful to our marriage when we began to consider how birth order affected our relationship.

Another opposite that greatly affects marriage is the issue of closeness and distance. While they are not opposites in the sense of personality characteristics, nevertheless this issue is a major part of a healthy marriage. We want and need togetherness. Healthy marriages happen when couples devote themselves to enhancing closeness. At the same time, we all need a certain amount of autonomy to go side-by-side with togetherness. We all cherish our space. Because we cannot be married and single at the same time, how to reshape our shared identity and, at the same, time affirm each person's uniqueness and individuality is an important balancing task of a healthy marriage.

What makes the closeness/distance factor so difficult is the complexity that is involved. The complexity arises when each spouse does not want or need the same amount of closeness or distance. Also, one spouse may want some distance at the exact same time his/her partner is feeling close. Some deal with stress by having time alone, while others find being with our spouse revives us. A spouse may have worked all day outside the home. Upon walking into the house at the end of a long day's work, he or she may desire some time alone. The other spouse may have worked all day in the home. At the end of the day, she or he may desire some closeness. It would be a lot easier if each spouse were on the same page when it comes to the timing of when they want space or togetherness.

How much distance a spouse may need or want depends on many factors. Most of these factors can be traced to our psychological history. For example, because of an early childhood experience where someone died or left, a "don't be close" message may be part of that person's personality and plays a significant role in the amount of distance needed and wanted.

How we deal with anger also has an effect on the closeness/distance issue. When conflict arises, we naturally feel distant from our spouse. The time that elapses before we want to return to closeness varies from spouse to spouse. For example, the wife may be ready to return to closeness at the same time the husband needs more time and distance. The wife responds by returning to feelings of distance and then is not ready for closeness when the husband is ready. The amount of time may be determined more by emotions than the issue that precipitated the conflict.

Whether or not it is acceptable for couples to have secrets from each other is related to the distance and closeness issue. Should couples have secrets from each other? My answer is yes and no. It depends. It depends on what each couple decides is okay. It depends on how each spouse deals with the matter of trust and suspicion. More than likely it will depend on the nature of the secret. I do not think a hard and fast rule should be established. The issue of having secrets will vary from couple to couple.

Of course, the issue of closeness/distance plays a major role in lovemaking. When we make love, we are close to our spouse, physically if not emotionally. A husband and/or wife will often create distance following lovemaking. Usually this is outside their awareness. Often the decision to have space is not acted upon until several hours or even days after the lovemaking. Sometimes the distance may be expressed by creating a minor fight. If the issue of distance/closeness, as it relates to lovemaking, is not discussed, the result is often accompanied by feelings of rejection which, in turn, creates more distance.

The primary reason for my feelings of distance from Elaine comes under the category of *unknown*. Many times I feel unable to identify the cause of the distant feeling. I will try to pin it on something she said or did not say or something I did or did not do. I am beginning to think my feeling distant has more to do with my biological make-up than any specific event. I have learned to accept my feelings are just that, feelings. They do not last and I return to feeling close to Elaine.

Acknowledging when you are feeling distant and sharing this with your spouse are probably more important then identifying the reasons for feeling distant.

The boundary lines between distance and closeness need to be continually redrawn and redefined. The lines will vary from marriage to marriage. Marriages are enhanced when the issue of closeness and distance is seen as a valuable part of building married love. It is a loving act for couples to share when distance is wanted and know it is a normal part of marital love. The sharing avoids unnecessary feelings of rejection.

Some couples may identify so many opposite characteristics that they will question whether they are compatible. But asking whether you are incompatible is the wrong question. The better question is: How can we turn our opposite personality characteristic into an advantage? This may call for re-working the original marriage contract to some degree.

Of course, most couples have similar personality characteristics. They like the same things. But these common personality traits can also become a source of tension in a marriage. When our spouse shares a similar personality trait we do not like about ourselves we are continually reminded of it. Boredom often happens as the result of two persons being alike. Being attracted to what is new and exciting seems to be part of human nature. Recognizing how personality similarities might lead to boredom can be helpful as couples examine their relationship.

Recently I was watching a rerun of a 1970's sitcom. The couple had been married for one year and had a baby. The scene was in the counselor's office. They were experiencing trouble in their marriage. The counselor asked them to share what they saw as the problem. The woman began by pointing out that her husband never wanted to do anything new. He was a man of habit. He did everything the same. She, on the other hand, wanted to take risks and experience new things. He admitted he liked to stay at home, just relax and not have to be doing something. This was especially true in light of the fact that his job had lots of stress.

The next scene was in their home. The wife was taking the baby to the park and asked if he wanted to come. He responded by suggesting they take the baby to a different park. He was trying to branch out and not do things the same as she had accused him. The wife said she did not want to go to a different park. She liked the park she had always gone to because it was familiar.

I was reminded how we may want our spouse to be different. In this case, she wanted her husband to not always do the same thing over and over. Yet there was a part of her that also wanted sameness. And while he wanted sameness, there was a part of him that wanted to venture outside the box.

In some ways your spouse is different from you. So what? Would you really expect this not to be the case? In this day and age of computers, many are finding their life partner on internet dating websites. You can easily search for someone who has common interests, someone who shares your values and goals. Finding someone who is like you is important. But what would happen if, when you meet this person, you spend time not just talking about your similarities, but talking about how you are different. Then discuss how the differences may impede your relationship or add to its vitality and health.

Every one of us enters a relationship with quirks, idiosyncrasies, flaws, weirdness, annoying habits, deficiencies and eccentricities. Some of these characteristics are similar to our spouse. Some are opposite. Some would best be described as simply different. We must all learn to celebrate our differences and make them work for us.

In one of the classrooms in our church there is a picture of a dog and cat. They are lying on the ground, embracing each other. Below the picture are these words: "It is because we're so different from each other that we have so much to share."

QUESTIONS FOR PERSONAL REFLECTION AND

DISCUSSION WITH YOUR SPOUSE

Kiss 1: Share the personality characteristics that originally drew you together. Share how they sometimes provoke tension in your marriage.

Kiss 2: Go through the lists of opposites and talk about which ones apply to your marriage. How can you translate an opposite personality characteristic into something positive?

Kiss 3: Share the ways you think you are different from your spouse because you are a member of the opposite sex.

Kiss 4: Discuss how your language of love differs from your spouse.

Kiss 5: Talk openly about the issue(s) of closeness and distance as it relates to your experience. What needs to take place in order for the closeness/distance issue to become a positive rather than a negative?

Kiss 6: Share the ways you are similar. How might these similarities create a degree of tension? How do these similarities enhance your relationship?

KISS 7: Write down role expectations for yourself and your spouse. Which ones have changed over the years? Which ones would you like to change? How has your upbringing affected your answers?

9

How To Say, I Love You

Most couples declare "I love you" to one another on a daily basis. As the years go by, it becomes a habitual way to end a conversation or part ways; but what are we really saying?

It might seem like a sweet, enduring sign off; but "I love you" can sound hollow when it isn't accompanied by genuine caring, listening and encouragement. Words, no matter how kind, do not take the place of being "present" in a relationship.

Marriage counselors frequently hear these words: "My wife/husband doesn't listen to me." "Oh I listen to her. I just don't agree with what she's saying. She just thinks I am not listening. Besides, she can talk endlessly about something and never focus on the main point." "Oh, I listen to him. He just doesn't think I do, because he is so busy trying to convince me he is right."

The purpose of this chapter is to assist you in the art and skill of effective marriage communication, the kind of communication that undeniably says, "I love you."

Love listening, as I am calling it, enables our spouse to experience our love as we listen carefully to what she/he is saying and feeling. The communication skill of love listening may be the most powerful skill a couple can learn. Saying "I love you", by listening to your spouse, takes a significant amount of energy and thought.

Morris and Maureen came for counseling. I determined their problems would be alleviated by improved communication. I spent a considerable amount of time helping them communicate about their problems, using the communication skills that are shared in this chapter. With my assistance, they were able to use the communication skills while in my office. But when they did the skills at home, they said, "We don't do very well. We seem to end up in an argument. Besides, it was difficult to do. We are so busy."

I realized many of the issues we have examined in previous chapters were getting in the way of using their communication skills. Before the communication skills could be productive, Morris and Maureen needed to spend some time in honest self-examination, including their insecurities as well as the barriers that were undermining their efforts to improve their communication. If couples do not look carefully at what is stopping them from practicing good communication skills, all the knowledge about improving communication will be sabotaged.

Couples will tell me they can't find time for making communication a priority, but rarely have they truly explored why it is not a priority. Here is a list of barriers to communication; you may have others to add to the list:

- We have talked about a particular issue before. Nothing changes, so why give it so much time and effort?
- We talk a lot. Doing the communication exercises seems so repetitive. I already know what my spouse thinks about almost every issue/topic.
- I don't see the importance of setting up a time to talk. It seems too rigid.
- Sometimes it is best to leave well enough alone. Why rock the boat when things are not that bad in our marriage?
- We are so busy. We rarely have the time and energy it takes to do the kind of communication you suggested. Besides, schedules are altered by parents' visits, changes in work, children's activities, household chores, finances, etc . . .

- It seems when we try to communicate, we never solve anything.
- My spouse doesn't do it right. He/she keeps interrupting and making statements rather than asking questions.
- Many couples feel vulnerable when they apply good communication skills to their relationship. This vulnerability may, subconsciously or consciously, be a barrier.
- When we try to do our communication skills, it seems as if one or both of us get defensive. We want to be right.
- It is difficult to wait for my turn to talk. I am afraid I will forget what I wanted to say.
- When my spouse is talking, I find myself thinking of what I want to say and, therefore, don't do a good job of listening.
- My spouse criticizes the way I do the communication exercise.
- My spouse wants to give advice instead of listening to what I have to say.
- My spouse wants to be in control and does not wait until I am through talking.
- When I share feelings, my spouse becomes uncomfortable. I notice my spouse's mind beginning to wander.
- When a quick answer to the problem is not forthcoming, my spouse turns off.
- My husband/wife has difficulty talking about feelings, and so we get bogged down by sharing opinions.
- This communication stuff takes a lot of time and energy. When my day is over, I am spent.
- It feels like I am the only one who initiates doing our communication skills.
- Communicating with my spouse is risky. We may get into areas which will produce tension.
- Our schedules are so different. When I am ready to talk, he/she is at a different point.
- We had an argument. I'm not in the mood to talk, and I'm surely am not in the mood to set a time to talk.

The main barrier I hear as a counselor is: "We are so busy with other things. We don't have time or take time to do our communication exercise." Preoccupation with issues other than our marriage is a decision we make. Being busy is a choice. The decision and choice are usually the result of a subconscious or conscious resistance to what it takes to apply good communication skills. Unless the reasons for the resistance are identified, being busy will continue to be seen as a reason rather than an excuse.

Now let's review effective communication skills. I say "review" because for many of you good communication skills are nothing new. I know men and women who have been trained to use some of these communication skills at their place of employment.

I am suggesting three ways for improving communication in a marriage.

I. Love Listening. There are three steps for effective love listening:

Step One: Set aside 20 minutes for what I call a 10 and 10. During the twenty minutes, eliminate all potential distractions such as phone, children and television. Each spouse will talk for 10 minutes while your partner listens, using steps two and three. The listener is also the timer. Switch roles after the 10 minutes.

It has been important for Elaine and me to be very intentional about setting aside time for our 10 and 10 sessions. We know about effective communication skills, but we are not very good at implementing them in our everyday relationship. Why not? We are selfish, self-centered, lazy and preoccupied with other things, to name a few of our reasons/excuses. Our salvation comes from being intentional in establishing a specific time for doing communication skills. Being intentional is quite different from casual, everyday communication. While we are not always successful in how and when we do our 10 and 10, nevertheless we have increased our love and decreased our conflicts by being intentional in establishing a specific time.

Being intentional about setting aside a time has not always been easy. In addition to busy schedules, she is a night person and I am a morning person. Opposites attract. She wants to do a 10 and 10 at night when I am tired and ready to sleep. I prefer the morning. If we are not intentional about deciding together when to do our love listening, we end up doing it badly or not doing it.

I know of couples who do a 10 and 10 once a day. Others prefer twice a week or once a week. Once a month is better than nothing. It is important for couples to agree together on the frequency for doing their love listening.

A suggestion that has helped Elaine and me is to stop our dialogue after the 20 minutes are completed, even if there is more to be said. There are several reasons for stopping after twenty minutes. First, it takes mental energy to listen to each other in the manner suggested in steps two and three. As with any activity, we tend to slack off when we get tired or weary. We are not at our best. Second, we can always set aside as many 10 and 10 time periods as we want. Having time to think about the topic and come back to it often results in a more productive experience. Third, going beyond the pre-defined time limit can result in compromising steps two and three. One or both partners will often resort to talking rather than using their listening skills. Fourth, when the topic being discussed is a difficult one, Elaine and I have found going beyond 20 minutes turns out to be counterproductive and unnecessarily elevates tension. We can always come back to the issue. When we come back to the issue at a later time, we increase the chances of our conversation being more productive and loving.

What do you talk about? I suggest when you are first beginning, avoid controversial topics. Elaine and I have found that simply asking each other to share the highs and lows of our day opens doors for all the conversation we need. "What was your most positive and negative feeling today" is also a good starter question. For aid with things to talk about, bring up the website, *ematrimony.com* and click "dialogue" "questions." There are more the 36,000 questions from which to choose.

Step Two: Tell your spouse what you heard him/her saying.

Healthy communication is more than exchanging thoughts. It begins with listening. We communicate we are truly listening and not just going through the motions when we let our spouse know we heard what he/she said.

Elaine speaks. She makes a statement. I speak and make a statement. She responds with another statement and I respond in like manner. We are like two ships passing in the night. We transfer information to each other hoping our spouse will hear and understand what we are saying. Frequently, my statements are intended to get Elaine to see my point of view, to agree with me. I tell myself, if this happens, the issue would be settled. Passing on information is important in a marriage, but it does not mean communication has taken place and certainly does not settle the issue(s). In the communication pattern where Elaine speaks and I speak, we assume the other is listening. Indeed, I may be listening; but does she *feel* I am listening?

Step two may be done by repeating the exact words your spouse has said or by paraphrasing what you heard. For me, it is best to simply repeat Elaine's words and follow it with, "Is this what you are saying?" or "Did I hear you correctly?" More than likely your spouse will let you know if you were listening, and then continue talking.

Step two opens the door in case what Elaine said is not really what she wanted to talk about. If I respond with a statement, I may not get to the essence of what she is really saying. Frequently, behind her words there is a wealth of unexpressed thoughts and feelings. By reflecting back what I heard her say, an entirely different topic may emerge, different from the one she initially communicated. Step two holds potential for getting at the depth of what she is feeling and thinking.

I recall the time when I came home from work. Elaine asked me if I had taken out the trash. I impatiently responded, "I will do it when I am good and ready." Elaine was smart enough to know the issue was not the trash. She responded, "I hear you saying you will take out the trash when you get ready. Am I right?" "You got it," I said. "And you are not ready now, did I hear you correctly?" She did not say anything for a few moments. Because I felt she heard me, in a few moments I began to share my frustrations about the committee meeting at the church and how one person single-handedly turned the meeting into a disaster. Had Elaine focused on my response to the trash issue, I would not have gotten to the real issue. Through her using step two of love listening, I began to share what was really going on in me rather than continue on the trash issue.

Step two also enables me to really hear what I have just said. When Elaine repeats back to me what I said, I often realize it is not what I meant or wanted to say. By Elaine using step two, I am able to clarify my thoughts and feelings.

Often, in response to step two, your spouse may say, "Yes, you heard me but . . ." "Yes, but" need not be taken as criticism of your listening skills, but rather an indicator that there is more your spouse has to say. Respond to "yes, but" as an invitation to continue listening.

My first experience with this reflective listening style was in a seminary pastoral care class. I was a bit skeptical, but I had to give it a try. It was an assignment.

I was assigned to do visiting on a TB floor of a local hospital in Dallas. I walked into a patient's room. A very large woman sat in the chair next to the bed. I had decided I would do what I had been taught without wavering one bit. I began the conversation: "How are you doing." "Fine," she said without looking up. Her tone of voice was harsh and short. "I hear you saying you are doing fine?" "That's what I said." "I hear you saying, that's what you said?" "You got it." "I hear you saying I have got it." I was determined to do exactly what my professor said I should do, even though the dialogue felt contrived, and I felt like an idiot. Maybe I could prove to my professor that he was wrong.

At this point, she stopped talking, seemingly disgusted with me and the way the conversation was going. She seemed unwilling to respond to this stranger who was intent on repeating everything she said. I decided to let the silence go on for awhile. I was taught silence is good. But she did not speak. I was convinced I could sit there for an hour and nothing would happen. So I decided to try again. "I asked you how you were doing and you said, "fine". Somehow I get the feeling you are not doing all that hot." "You can say that again." "I hear you saying that I can say that again." You get the idea. I was determined to do exactly what I was taught. For me it was an experiment to see if this reflective/love listening thing really worked. I was on a mission. I used my "technique" of active listening for the entire hour. I left and went back to the dorm to write up my experience. I was anxious to let the professor know it did not work.

The next week I returned to my hospital assignment. As I was walking down the hall, a nurse stopped me. "Are you the chaplain from the seminary?" she asked. "That's me," I replied. "Did you visit Mrs. Smith in room 305 last week?" "I was not sure of her name, but I did visit the lady in 305." The nurse went on to inform me that Mrs. Smith had been depressed for months and was a problem to all the nurses. She complained constantly, and her anger spilled over throughout the day to everyone who had contact with her. The nurse said to me, "What did you do? Her attitude has changed. She does not seem as depressed and is actually quite pleasant." The nurse told me she liked Mrs. Smith's new attitude. The nurse had asked Mrs. Smith what happened. Mrs. Smith responded, "A man came to visit me; and, for the first time, I felt someone really cared about me."

I, of course, was amazed. I felt obligated to inform my professor and classmates this kind of listening works, if by "works" you mean communicates caring.

When it comes to incorporating step two with your spouse, you can be more original then simply repeating, "I hear you saying." There are many creative ways to let your spouse know you are listening to what he/she is saying, thereby conveying your care and love. Step two communicates to your spouse that you are willing to listen without interruption, evaluation or judgment. Who would not welcome such an experience and receive it as genuine caring? Yes, love listening takes effort. It is not always easy to do, especially when what we are hearing pushes our hot buttons.

Here is an example of a typical non-communication conversation Elaine and I have had many times. I follow with an example that incorporates step two.

Virgil: "You are late again. I can't believe it. You are so insensitive to me and my schedule."

Elaine: "I had to respond to an important phone call. I couldn't help it. Besides I wasn't that late."

V. "You always have some excuse for being late. You never plan ahead or think."

E. "I don't know why you get so upset. It's not that big of a deal."

At this point, the conversation usually stops. We both are mad and go our separate ways or continue our activity without talking. Here is how the conversation might take place when step two is applied.

Virgil. "You are late again. I can't believe it. You are so insensitive to me and my schedule."

Elaine: "You are upset that I am late and feel I am being insensitive to you and your schedule."

V. "That's right. I suppose you have another lame excuse."

E. "You feel when I am late I usually offer lame excuses."

(The normal response would be for her to offer reasons for being late. This would be irrelevant to what was going on in me.)

V. "You got that right."

E. "You feel when I make excuses I am being even more insensitive to you." (Notice how Elaine came back to a word I had used, insensitive.)

V. "Don't you think you are being insensitive to my schedule?"

E. "I know you feel I am being insensitive to your schedule."

V. "If you know that, then why do you continue being late?"

E. "You would think if I was more sensitive to you I would not continue being late. Am I hearing you?"

V. "Well, don't you think that would be the case?"(Again, notice she did not fall into the trap of answering my question.)

E. "You feel I would not continue being late if I were more sensitive to you." (Notice how Elaine comes back to the key issue, which is not being late but insensitivity.)

V. "Well, you are being insensitive."

E. "You feel I am being insensitive to you and your schedule."

At this point in the conversation I am still mad, but the intensity has lessened because I feel she is hearing me. Letting me know she is listening to my feelings led to a more positive outcome than how this conversation usually happens. It felt good and different when she was using love listening rather than the usual pattern of defending herself.

The issue of her being late was not solved, but the more important issue surfaced when Elaine implemented step two. The real issue is feeling she is insensitive to me. Through some counseling I came to understand I was feeling left out and lonely. I covered this lonely feeling with anger. I would not have made it to the real issue and to my feelings without her listening to me by using step two.

My wife has told me it sometimes feels elementary to simply repeat back to me what she just heard. For her, step two feels rote and contrived. Initially repeating what your spouse says may feel awkward, especially when what was said is obvious. At the same time, it is an important way for you and your spouse to insure that listening is happening, rather than forming your response and leaving your spouse to wonder if he/she has been heard. When my wife repeats what I have said, I feel I have been heard. This is more important than whether she agrees or disagrees.

Last week, Elaine and I got into a conversation that was heading in the direction of an argument. She expressed an opinion with which I disagreed. I expressed my opinion. She responded with an even stronger expression of her idea about the subject. I elevated my response to her response. We both were getting angry. At some point in the discussion, Elaine said, "I hear you saying that . . ." When she let me know she heard what I said, I could feel my whole body change. I was not as tense. I realized she had heard my ideas even though she showed no sign of changing her opinion. The argument began to subside. I no longer had the need to convince her that I was right. Evidently, having the assurance she heard my point of view was more important than her agreeing with me.

Step two works best when couples set aside their intentional dialogue time and share their 10 and 10. It may be feel redundant when the topic is simply part of everyday conversation. Step two may feel unnecessary when the topic is not filled with emotion. For example, if you are sharing about your day, it may feel ridiculous to repeat what your spouse is saying. But when the topic is filled with potential conflict and tension, step two is essential. If we have not learned step two when talking about non-threatening topics, it may be difficult to do when it comes to those difficult and threatening topics. Step two frequently results in our partner continuing to share. In some cases when step two is used, step three may even become unnecessary.

When your spouse indicates that you have heard what he/she is saying, proceed to step three. Step three communicates you are listening and want to hear more.

Step Three: Give your spouse an open-ended statement and/or question.

An open-ended statement or question invites and encourages your spouse to say more about the issue/topic.

I have found open-ended questions generate better communication than statements. Statements give information, present an opinion and offer suggestions. Statements are frequently used to motivate our spouse to do what we think is best and/or right. Therefore, statements often result in responses that are unhelpful. This is especially true when communication involves issues that are difficult and complex.

Statements are often received as advice. I give couples this advice: Don't give advice to your spouse. While it is obvious there are times when advice is welcomed and needed, advice in a marriage is a prescription for creating tension. Advice often communicates the message that you don't respect your spouse's intelligence to figure things out. You will figure it out for your spouse. Advice may communicate to your spouse, "You do not have the capability to solve problems. I will solve your problems for you." Certainly you don't want to say, "You are a problem."

I can give you advice and you can give me advice, and the same dynamic will not happen as it does in a marriage relationship. Remember when you were a small child? You got lots of advice. That is the nature of a parent-to-child relationship. As we grew up there was plenty of advice. At the age of 18, you left home. You felt free from having to receive advice. In a family relationship of husband and wife, we inevitably associate advice-giving with what we felt in our family as a child. When our spouse gives us advice, we resurrect those childhood feelings that took place when our parents gave us advice. Nobody wants to be married to a parent, nor do we want our spouse feeling like a child. Advice is often associated with criticism, even if that is not the intent.

I have been asked, "What if my spouse asks for advice?" Be hesitant. Before making a statement or giving advice, I would check out whether he or she really wants advice. This can be done by using steps two and three. If your spouse says, "What do you think I should do?," using step two might sound something like, "I hear you asking me to tell you what you should do?" More than likely the response will be, "Well, not really. I just wanted . . ." When your spouse asks for advice, step three might sound like, "What ideas and options have you been thinking about?"

I recall a time when Elaine came home after experiencing pain and conflict at her work. She explained the situation. I listened and invited her to share her pain. I was determined to practice what I preached and not try to fix her pain or solve the situation. After a time, she said to me, "Virgil, you are good with people. What would you do in this situation? I need your advice." Against my better judgment, I proceeded to offer my advice. The result was not desirable. A minor argument followed. What she needed and wanted was to share her feelings. She did not really want me to fix her. She is smart and competent and very capable of solving the situation. She needed me to ask questions that enabled her to think clearly about what was needed in order to deal with a difficult situation. Open-ended questions say, "I am here to share your pain, rather than take your pain away and/or try to fix it." You can guess the response when your spouse feels you are trying to fix him/her.

The following story illustrates the loving things that happen when we avoid using communication skills to solve or fix a problem.

Ace and Alie were having some tension in their marriage. The tension was largely in response to problems Ace and Alie were having with their two children. This was a second marriage for both. The children were from the wife's previous marriage. Both children were in grade school when they were married and now were teenagers. Both kids had been doing and saying things that were unacceptable to the parents. Some of the things they were doing scared the parents. The parents had tried everything they knew to help improve the situation. The teenagers' behavior and attitude were having a negative affect on the marriage.

After they shared story with me, I said to Alie, "What do you want from your husband in this situation? He has just said he did not know what to do. What do you expect him to do?" Her response was, "I don't expect him to do anything. I simply want him to be there for me, to love and support me." Ace immediately began to weep, got up and left the room. The wife asked, "Where is he going? What's wrong with him?" I responded, "I don't know for sure, but he will be back." In a few minutes Ace returned. I asked him, "Would you like to share what is going on in you right now?" He began to share that the tears were an expression of relief. He had been living under the burden that as the step-father he was expected to do something to fix and solve the children's problems. He had assumed his wife expected him to intervene and come up with an answer to solve the teenagers' unacceptable behavior. When his wife told him all she wanted from him was love and support, he was overwhelmed with relief. All she wanted was for him to be with her and listen to her pain, frustration and fear. As their counselor, I was more successful in helping them use their communication skills when they both realized the purpose was not to solve or fix a problem.

In using step three, some statements are well intended but are not open-ended. For example, "You'd be better off if you think more positive." "Don't worry about it. Things will get better." These two statements give an opinion rather than invite more sharing.

Consider this statement: "Honey, I think it would be good for us to take some time and consider all the options." Now think about how an open-ended question might produce a different and better response. "Honey, what would happen if we took some time and considered all the options?" Even this question comes close to being a statement. An even better open-ended question might be, "Tell me what you have been thinking as you consider the various options?"

Open-ended questions work better than statements in encouraging your spouse to share more about an issue and express feelings.

An open-ended question cannot be answered with a yes or no. For example, your spouse may say to you, "I don't know whether I should tell my parents or just wait and see what happens." A yes or no question would be, "Do you think it is best to be direct with your parents?" An open-ended-question might be, "What do you think would be the result of waiting or being direct?" "How do you feel about telling your parents?"

A question that begins with "why" is often not received as open-ended. For example, "Why do you feel that way?" A more inviting question might be, "How do you feel when that happens?"

Asking your spouse, "How was your day?" appears to be an open-ended question, but often gets a one-word answer, "ok" or "fine." "Tell me about your day" is more invitational and open-ended.

In using step three, I have found it is helpful to pick out a key word Elaine has used that I recognize is filled with meaning. I then ask her to tell me more about what she meant when she used that word.

Read the following dialogue. With your spouse, discuss how steps two and three can improve your communication skills.

"How was your day?"
"Fine."
"Your day was fine?"
"Yes, it was ok."

(Some might be inclined to respond, "I guess we all have days that are just ok." Again, this is a statement that may not invite our spouse to continue and tell us more.)

"I am not sure what you mean by ok. What do you mean?"
"I mean it was ok, not too bad or too good. Just ok. You know."
"I hear you saying it was not too bad or too good. I am still not sure what that means for you. I would like to know more. Maybe you could share the bad parts and the good parts."
"Well, you know my boss. He never seems to be satisfied."

"Your boss is never satisfied?"
"Yea, he expects me to get those plans done in a matter of hours when in reality it takes me days."

"It takes much more than a couple of hours for you to get those plans done? Am I hearing you correctly?"

"Yes."

"How do you feel when the boss lays those expectations on you?"

"I feel . . . I'm not sure how I feel."

"You are not sure how you feel?"

"Yea, I guess I feel pressure and I don't like that."

"I know I don't like pressure either. How do you deal with that pressure?"

"Not very well."

"Tell me more of how you think the pressure affects what is going on in your life."

The spouse repeated the word "pressure" in order to encourage more sharing about the feelings associated with pressure. Helping identify the feelings that go along with pressure was significant to the listening process.

One person responded to my thoughts about the potentially negative aspects of making statements: "What about giving your spouse reassuring statements, such as 'Everything is going to be alright' or 'Don't worry' or 'I will be by your side' or 'God will provide strength for making it through this experience?'" I suggest reassuring statements be postponed until you are confident your spouse feels he/she has been heard. Giving reassuring statements prematurely, before you have done steps two and three, may leave your spouse feeling cut off. If a spouse rushes into statements of reassurance without first listening, your partner may not feel like sharing more on the topic. When we do a good job of listening to our spouse, reassuring words and actions will be received and welcomed. In fact, fully listening to your spouse may communicate reassurance more than words of reassurance.

I recall visiting with a couple who came to me for counseling. I talked with them about listening skills. His wife came home and began to complain about her job. He quickly remembered he was to listen by letting her know he heard what she was saying and then to ask open-ended questions. At one point in the conversation, he made this *statement* which he thought was a good one: "I am here to help you." The word, "help," triggered the little child in the wife and she put a parent face on him. She was an intelligent woman and did not need his help, nor was she asking for it. She felt cut off and protected. She was asking him to listen and let her vent.

Remember, the purpose of using good communication skills is not for solving problems. If problems become solved as the result of good communication, that is a wonderful side benefit. But I would caution couples about expecting good communication to solve marital problems.

If communication is not for solving problems, then what is the purpose? The primary purpose is for increasing closeness and love.

Elaine and I have numerous issues that, in our judgment, are not solvable. Using our communication skills has not solved the problem. What has taken place is an increased understanding of what the other thinks and feels about an issue. This increased understanding has greatly reduced our arguments, which in turn has increased our love in the midst of our disagreements.

Another purpose of steps two and three is to invite your spouse to "throw up." Remember when you were a child and had a stomach ache. When you vomited you felt better. Cleaning up the vomit was the ultimate loving act of your parents. I find what Elaine and I need is time to "throw up" our feelings and thoughts and know someone cares. It may not smell good, but your spouse will feel better. Step two communicates to our lover that we are willing to receive and clean up their emotional vomit. This certainly communicates the message, I love you. I am here to share your pain, not take it away.

Several years ago I had experienced some pain and conflict at work. When I walked into the house, Elaine sensed something was wrong. She asked me to share. After sharing the pain I was feeling, she made astute observations about the situation at my work. She lovingly tried to ease my pain with reassuring words and suggestions on how to handle the situation.

It is normal to want our spouse to feel good. I love Elaine for wanting to ease my pain with reassuring words and perceptive observations. But for me, easing my pain comes through listening to me and my feelings. I do not feel she is listening to me when she makes statements, no matter how reassuring her words or how accurate her observations

Elaine gets on me for not sharing enough of my feelings. When she does steps two and three, I find myself more willing to talk because I know I will not be interrupted or misunderstood.

I want to address the issue of being interrupted that is often a misunderstanding some couples may have when doing their 10 and 10, especially using step two.

It had been about three years since Nate and Nora came to me for counseling. Their issue was related to how they were different. They had married an "opposite." When they arrived I asked, "What is the agenda? Why have you come?" Nora began, "We are having difficulty with our communication skills." I replied, "Tell me what is happening." "I don't know," said Nora. "We have gotten lax and often get into an argument instead of really communicating."

After asking some questions about how they were doing their 10 and 10, I suggested they do one and I would be their coach. Nora started talking and Nate listened. What she said to Nate was somewhat emotionally charged. After Nora talked for about 30 seconds, I told Nate to interrupt her and tell her what he heard her saying. Nate responded, "I didn't think it was good to interrupt. As long as she was expressing herself, I should let her talk until she was finished and then tell her what I heard her saying."

I shared that, when I listen to Elaine, it is difficult for me to remember what she has said if she talks much more than 30-40 seconds at a time, especially if it is an emotional issue. "It is OK," I said, "and, in fact helpful to interrupt your partner. This is an important way of communicating that you are listening. Your spouse can always pick up on where he/she left off. I find it difficult listening to Elaine for one or two minutes and do a good job of letting her know I heard what she was saying." I would suggest interrupting at the end of a sentence might be best.

My suggestions were helpful to Nate and Nora. Also, they had been doing their 10 and 10 during an argument. I reminded them that a 10 and 10 needed to be an intentional, planned time, certainly after the feelings of an argument had subsided.

II. Writing a Letter. The focus thus far has been on face-to-face, verbal communication. Another form of communication that has helped our marriage is writing a letter to each other.

Start by agreeing upon a topic. Write for a pre-determined amount of time. Ten minutes is a good time period. Write your letters in separate locations. This eliminates noticing your spouse is writing more or less, faster or slower.

Come together and exchange your letters. This may be immediately after you write or later in the day. Some couples find it helpful to write at their convenience during the day and then exchange letters at an agreed upon time. Some couples will read the letter silently and then discuss. Other couples find it helpful to read a letter out loud.

The "hot pen" theory of writing is helpful. Write without regard for spelling, punctuation and penmanship. Focus on "I" statements rather than "you" statements. This minimizes judging and criticizing. Remember the purpose is not to solve an issue but to increase communication and caring.

Writing, versus face-to-face dialogue, is an excellent opportunity to practice sharing and describing feelings as emphasized in chapter five.

When Elaine and I talk to each other, our non-verbal communication often gets in the way, such as a sigh, a look or a frown. Writing bypasses these non-verbals. We can organize our thoughts and feel more assured we have said what we wanted to say.

I have written a letter to Elaine and then did not give her the letter. I simply needed to get something off my chest. I felt better after I wrote the letter. By writing, I can recognize and avoid trigger words that are uncalled for and unhelpful, such as "you always" or "you never."

I have had times in my marriage when I want to express myself to Elaine face-to-face, but stopped myself for some unknown reason. Writing helped me say what I wanted to say.

III. Give compliments.

Words of praise and appreciation are nourishment to a marriage and helpful in effective communication. We feel close to someone who affirms us. Through praise and compliments we let our spouse know we are not, after all the years, taking him/her for granted.

As you give your spouse praise and compliments, consider these words of caution.

Caution One: Some people have difficulty receiving compliments and praise. This is usually the result of their psychological history. We assume praise and compliments will be received positively. But words of affirmation and appreciation can provoke unsettling feelings in some people. For example, when someone does not feel deserving of the compliment, they may say, "It wasn't really that big of a deal. You're just saying that to make me feel better." When a person rebuffs a compliment, the giver will be reluctant to give compliments in the future. It would be helpful for couples to discuss how each receives compliments and praise.

Caution Two: We have noted how self-esteem is an essential prerequisite to good communication. Praise and compliments enhance self-esteem. When Elaine says good things about me, I feel good about myself. Be careful if and when your self-esteem is dependent upon your spouse's words of encouragement and praise. Remember, even if compliments enhance self-esteem, you are not responsible for your spouse's self-esteem. You are in a precarious position if your self-esteem is dependent upon another's affirmation and praise.

Caution Three: Compliments and praise can be a way of patronizing your spouse. Discuss with your spouse whether this is the case in your marriage. For example, if the compliment has to do with how your spouse has improved, your spouse may take it as your saying he/she needed to improve. This may be received as advice and criticism rather than a compliment. Rather than enhancing self-esteem some words of praise and compliment may communicate one spouse is superior.

Caution Four: Are your compliments a way to get what you want, for example sex, new clothes, furniture or . . . ? This turns words of praise and appreciation into manipulation. Trying to motivate your spouse with a compliment will get mixed results.

Caution Five: Words of praise and affirmation can be a way to avoid dealing with conflict and tension. Ask yourself whether you are complimenting your spouse as a way to steer clear of your feelings.

Caution Six: Take careful note whether your compliment is for something your spouse accomplished or achieved or simply for who he/she is. It is the difference between feeling accepted, period, rather than being accepted if and when I do something. It is a matter of communicating conditional love versus unconditional love.

Caution Seven: Precede any words of appreciation, affirmation and praise with the communication skills mentioned in this chapter. Our spouse will be more receptive to our compliments *after* we have lovingly listened to them.

Communication is an art, especially asking open-ended questions. Listening to your spouse using steps two and three is a skill we can learn. This art is relatively new to most of us. We did not experience it growing up, nor was it taught to us in our formal education. Like any new task or skill there is a learning curve. It will take time to learn. It will take practice. It will include trial and error. Decide as a couple to be patient with each other as you learn the art of good marital communication.

I suggest you make evaluation part of your 10 and 10 sessions. The purpose of the evaluation is to improve on the skill. Avoid being critical of how your spouse did or did not do steps two and three. Avoid pointing out that your spouse is sharing a thought, not a feeling. As with any learning experience, progress may be slower than you or your spouse wants. Be patient. Sometimes it is difficult to change long-established patterns.

I recall the words of Scott Peck in his best selling book, *The Road Less Traveled.*

"Listening well is an exercise of attention and by necessity hard work. It is because they do not realize this or because they are not willing to do the work that most people do not listen well. True listening, no matter how brief, requires tremendous effort. First of all, it requires total concentration. You cannot truly listen to anyone and do anything else at the same time. If a parent (spouse) wants to truly listen, we must put aside everything else . . . If you are not willing to put aside everything else, including our own worries and preoccupations for such a time, then you are not willing to truly listen . . . True listening, total concentration on the other, is always a manifestation of love."

Every issue of marriage cries out for improved communication. Communicating openly and honestly about our insecurities brings closeness. Trust in a marriage is enhanced as we communicate about our psychological history. Communicating about our anger patterns will greatly improve married love.

Because effective and healthy communication is a skill and an art, we all need guidance and help. This is the emphasis of the following chapter.

QUESTIONS FOR PERSONAL REFLECTION AND DISCUSSION WITH YOUR SPOUSE

KISS 1: Share with your spouse any barriers that pertain to your communication.

KISS 2: Discuss the idea of being intentional about setting aside 20 minutes for implementing your communication skills. How often you would like to do a 10 and 10.

KISS 3: How can step two help your communication? What are your hesitations about doing step two?

KISS 4: Discuss the different results that occur when we make a statement to our spouse versus asking an open-ended question. Share a time when a statement had an adverse effect on your communication.

KISS 5: How do you respond to the idea that words of reassurance may get in the way of effective communication?

KISS 6: Share how and why giving advice can result in a negative response from your spouse. Share a time when this has happened.

KISS 7: Share your response to the idea that the purpose of communication is not for solving problems.

KISS 8: Compliment your spouse and discuss the seven cautions.

10

Establish the Habit of Making Love

Healthy choices lead to healthy habits. What habits have you as a couple established? If you are like most couples, you probably have some good and some bad.

The habit of brushing your teeth is important for preventing tooth decay. A wise couple learns to establish habits that prevent marriage decay. This does not look the same in every marriage, but there are some universal habits that work for most marriages.

The first line of defense against marriage decay is preventive maintenance. By taking steps to keep a marriage healthy, the marriage can run as smoothly as possible, for as long as possible. When the inevitable bumps do happen, your marriage has some built-in cushion.

Many times when a couple finally seeks marriage counseling, the original problem has spread into other areas, making the issues more difficult to treat. It doesn't always mean it is too late, but it does jeopardize progress towards healing.

Why would anyone who is concerned about their health not take advantage of the precautionary measures of early detection? For example, early detection is a major reason for the improvements in cancer treatment. If you have a pain and the pain does not go away, it is an intelligent decision to see a doctor. Even if it turns out to be minor and can easily be treated, it was smart to have it checked out

Early detection of problems is a smart way to keep the marriage healthy. When a problem arises in a marriage, even if it turns out to be minor and can easily be handled, it is an intelligent decision to invest in periodic checkups. Although there are no guarantees, regular checkups are important for a healthy body and a healthy marriage.

I suggest six habits for preventive maintenance that will insure early detection of marriage problems. These habits will help with your decision to KISS throughout your married life.

Habit 1: Set aside special and specific times for listening to each other, using the suggestions for effective communication provided in the previous chapter.

I know a couple who call their special time "staff meetings." When I was a pastor of a local church, we held weekly staff meetings. The purpose was to: a. lend support to each other as we went about our ministry; b. make sure communication lines were open and active; c. keep on top of issues and potential problems before they got out of hand.

Sometimes we wondered whether having a staff meeting each week was really necessary; but we found out when we missed a week, unwanted and unnecessary things happened that could have been avoided by having a staff meeting.

Holding weekly "staff" meetings as a couple provides an intentional time to support each other as we go about our busy schedules. Marriage staff meetings ensure communication lines are open and active. You will keep on top of potential problems in the family and marriage before they get out of hand. There were times Elaine and I allowed ourselves to say we were too busy and too tired. Unwanted and unnecessary things happened in our relationship that could have been avoided by having our weekly staff meeting.

Habit 2: Join a Marriage Support Group.

Elaine and I often question whether our marriage would be as strong as it is without the small group experiences we had over the years with other couples. The main thing the groups did for us was provide the discipline of working on our marriage twice a month. It felt good to know other couples were dealing with some of the same issues. The group often discussed issues we had not talked about sufficiently.

Local churches talk about the importance of family values. Yet, I am amazed that most local churches do not offer marriage groups. If your church does not provide this opportunity, consider starting your own group.

You can start a marriage support group using the following ideas:

A. As a couple first define your vision for a marriage support group. How often would you like the group to meet? How many couples would be in the group? I recommend from six or seven, no more than eight.

What would happen in the group? Who would lead the group? In our groups, we decided upon a resource and each couple took turns leading. Sometimes a couple would present a topic they found in an article from a newspaper or magazine. Other couples would read from a book on marriage. In addition to this book, there are many books written about how to improve your marriage. Bookstores, libraries and the Internet are full of many good marriage resources.

Each meeting would start with a presentation by the lead couple. The presentation may consist of a few minutes or 15 minutes. The presentation was followed by each couple being by themselves for a period of time and then returning to the total group for shared discussion. Sometimes we brought in an outside person for the input time. Sometimes we would separate men and women for the writing of a letter to our spouse about the evening topic, and then read and discuss our letters. Couples would then return to the group for sharing.

We found adjourning for the summer was helpful. We also found it helpful to ask for a nine-month commitment from group members. The commitment was that each person/couple would attend every session, unless sick or out-of-town and then they would notify someone in the group. The commitment would include confidentiality. What is said in the group remains in the group.

B. Share your vision with one or two other couples and invite them to join you in starting a group. Be sure your vision includes arrangement for childcare.

C. With the other couples, visit with your pastor and get his/her support. Be clear with your pastor what you mean by "support."

D. In a worship service, share your vision and invite others to join you. Be creative with the announcement. Use skit, video, personal testimony, etc. Do not make the announcement more than a minute. Share your vision and invitation to join a group through the normal channels for publicity in your church. Don't depend on announcements for getting couples to join your group. With another couple, go to the home of a couple who you think might be interested and personally invite them to be part of the marriage support group. Remind them that the group is not for marriages in trouble, but for making good marriages better.

Habit 3: Seek help from a counselor.

Several times throughout the course of our marriage, Elaine and I have gone to counseling as a preventative measure. Our marriage was not in trouble. We simply had an issue that was producing more tension than we wanted. Our communication skills were not getting us past the hurt we were giving to each other.

I consider myself to be a fairly good marriage counselor. However, I can give a couple good advice, but go home and not put it into action in my own marriage. This does not make me a hypocrite, but it does make me a sinner who needs help. I believe the advice I gave. I am too emotionally involved to always have a healthy perspective on what is happening in my marriage. Getting a third party perspective is an intelligent habit to use. The best counselors I know have had help from counseling.

For many people, there is a stigma attached to counseling. Some feel it is a sign of weakness, rather than a sign of strength and wisdom. Some resistance comes from having to admit there are problems in the marriage. Denial takes precedence over a good decision. Even if going to a counselor is for the purpose of maintenance and checkup, some are worried about what others will think.

How does one go about picking a counselor, given the fact some counselors are better than others? You may want to make some prior decisions, such as qualifications and whether you prefer a male or female. I would be cautious about qualifications. In general, level of education is a useful criterion. I know some counselors who are, in my judgment, very qualified but do not have the level of education some people define as essential. Getting recommendations from other couples, pastor or doctor may be helpful. Don't hesitate to shop around. If you go to one and she/he does not fit, try another.

One criterion I use for determining a "good" counselor is the length of time it takes to get what I want and need. If the purpose of the counseling is maintenance and early detection, a lengthy time period is not always necessary.

The degree to which counseling is helpful depends not only upon the counselor's ability, but also the attitude a couple brings to counseling. If you see a counselor and are not getting the results you want or expected, make sure you are being honest with yourself and your reasons for going for counseling. The problem may be your attitude and not the counselor's ability to help you. Your resistance may come from the counselor hitting a note you did not want to hear or play. The resistance may be subconscious or conscious.

I have had some couples come for counseling, and after a time I can discern the purpose of one or both was not to strengthen their marriage.

Eve and Stanley were one of those couples who came to me. Eve's purpose for coming to counseling was to end the marriage. Sometimes couples are aware this is the reason for seeking counseling. Most of the time they do not realize or acknowledge this is their purpose.

During the first session, Eve reported having difficulty loving Stanley because he did not share his feelings. I asked Stanley whether Eve was correct in her assessment of him. He said, "Yes, I have never been very good at sharing my feelings, but I am willing to learn."

During the second session I helped Stanley work on sharing his feelings. Eve watched and listened as Stanley began to identify and share his feelings. At the end of the second session, we set a time for a third session.

One day before the next counseling session, Stanley phoned me. "I guess we are going to cancel our counseling session with you. Eve has filed for divorce. She doesn't want to do any more counseling."

In a few days I got a chance to talk with Eve. Before talking with her, I had assumed her reason for stopping counseling might have to do with her resistance to Stanley sharing feelings. As is often the case, a spouse wants feelings to be shared; but when it happens he/she will see the partner as weak and needy. There is a need for a spouse to be strong. In talking with Eve, I realized she was feeling guilty about getting a divorce and the real reason for coming to counseling was to get permission to end the marriage. Some couples seek counseling as a way to have a guilt-free divorce. Eve could tell her friends, children and family that she at least tried.

Then there was Trina and Tony who came for counseling. They began the session by telling me they had seen another counselor who was not helpful. It did not take very long for me to realize they had expected the counselor to solve their problems. They were not ready to take responsibility for doing what it would take to heal the marriage. They were intent on spending the counseling session pointing to each other as being the cause of the problem.

You probably will be disappointed if you expect the counselor to do something *for* you. Good counselors will ask you the right questions that empower you to work on your feelings, thoughts and issues. Only you can heal yourself. When I have gone for counseling, good questions were more helpful in the short and long run than advice and suggestions. The counselor is simply a guide along your journey of self-examination.

A good counselor invites you to enter into a process rather than prescribing a pill for quick relief. For most marital problems, there is no quick fix, no easy answer. As a counselor I have, at times, stopped the counseling when I determined I was working harder than my client.

I have a friend who went to see his doctor. The doctor was a personal friend. The nurse came into the waiting room and informed him that the doctor had decided not to see him. "You've got to be kidding," said my friend. "No," said the nurse. "But why?" my friend asked with astonishment. The nurse informed him that until he stopped smoking the doctor would not treat him any longer. The doctor said, "Why should I break my back trying to help you when you seem to be breaking your back to stay unhealthy by smoking?"

In order for counseling to be helpful, you will need to work hard in the counseling session as well as doing the homework. By work I do not mean drudgery. I simply mean taking responsibility for getting what you need and want and not expecting the counselor to do something for you.

In addition, you probably will be disappointed if you expect counseling to be painless. A certain amount of pain is to be expected in the process of examining our insecurities.

In their helpful book, *Do I Have To Give Up Me To Be Loved By You?*, Drs. Jordan and Margaret Paul write:

"Although pain is unpleasant, and understandably something we would like to avoid, opening to pain is the only way we have to learn what it has to teach us. Pain is nature's way of calling attention to what needs attention. Though we may have learned to recognize physical pain as a signal of trouble, we seldom extend the analogy to emotional pain. We are not required to like being in pain. What's to like? But because exploring ourselves and our partner might bring up something painful, we must at least be willing to be in pain before we can learn about ourselves . . . Just as bodily pain accompanies the learning of physical skills, emotional pain is the price of acquiring genuine self-knowledge . . . When you refuse to experience the pain that goes with a given difficulty much of your energy goes into protecting against the pain, which robs you of the energy you need to deal decisively with the problem. Most

people prefer to stay bogged down in low-grade misery from which they can see no escape rather than use their pain as a catalyst to learn and change."

As we say in the world of sports, no pain, no gain.

A lot of time and money is wasted because couples do not intentionally begin the counseling session by presenting the main problem/issue. For example, one or both partners will talk endlessly about the issue they perceive is causing conflict. They resist dealing with the underlying issue/ cause. They resist conversation about what each person needs to change in order to make progress. You will probably have a negative response to any counselor if you are not committed to making changes in yourself.

I have had many couples come for counseling who genuinely want to save the marriage. They are willing to claim their part in the problem. But it quickly becomes evident they should have come years ago. A lot of hurt had been given and received over the years. This does not mean the situation is hopeless. It does mean a lot of work in counseling will be required.

I have always encouraged a person to seek counseling even if his/her spouse will not go. If one partner makes significant changes, often the marriage will take a turn for the better. Obviously, if both spouses come to counseling the chances for turning the marriage around are increased.

If you think counseling is too expensive, you may want to compare the emotional and financial expense of a divorce.

Habit 4: Periodically attend a marriage workshop/seminar. It is an excellent habit for preventive maintenance.

Our first exposure to a marriage workshop was Marriage Encounter. Marriage Encounter focuses on the one-on-one interaction between partners. We have also attended and led Marriage Enrichment seminars which focus both on the one-on-one interaction between partners along with interaction among couples attending the event.

The value of such events is to provide stimulus and tools for working on the various issues of marriage. It provides a setting away from kids, work and the house. This has a freeing effect needed for discussing crucial marriage issues. If you have difficulty finding such events, go online. You can find an event near you or some romantic, exotic location where you and your partner could travel.

One note of caution, these seminars/workshops are not recommended for marriages in trouble. They are for the care and maintenance of good marriages which have the normal ups and downs.

Habit 5: Grow and Nourish the Spiritual Dimension of Your Marriage.

God is waiting to be invited into your marriage. You need the extra power God provides to your love.

Elaine and I have found doing church to be a helpful habit. Our marriage has been strengthened through the support we receive from the habit of worship, study, fellowship and giving our time, money and talents. Review together chapters one and three. Chapter one speaks to how God's love will impact your married love. Chapter three emphasizes how prayer can nourish your marriage.

Habit 6: Face a Major Crisis.

After about 25 years of marriage, Elaine was diagnosed with cancer. Fortunately, it was treatable and with time she went into remission. The disease woke us up to what is important in life. We gained a new perspective on life and conflict. We began to see how many of the things we fought about were minor in light of what really matters. Of course, we continue to fight about minor issues; but, because of the disease and God's power, the fights are not as long or intense and are certainly less frequent.

Continually reminding yourselves of what really matters in life is a worthwhile habit. Keeping the beauty of life and committed love in proper perspective will bring new life and hope to your marriage. Keeping the truth that your love and life are a gift from God will bring renewed energy and commitment to your marriage.

These six habits for making love may be a source of power for changing yourself and your marriage relationship. I have intentionally used the word, "may." Elaine and I have made these habits part of our marriage for 49 years, and there has been minimal change in our basic personalities.

Since no marriage is perfect, the issue of *change* is an important topic for couples to address. If your marriage is a seven, how can you change it to an eight?

People vary in their opinions about whether we as adults can actually change our personalities. For most of us, changing attitudes and behavior comes slowly. It is not as if you wake up one morning and say to your spouse, "Honey, I have changed."

So, why implement these habits if they don't produce change? While our personalities have not changed much from when Elaine and I got married, some significant changes have taken place. Our communication has improved. We made a concerted effort to identify and share feelings. Becoming aware of our insecurities and differences has led us to accepting each other as we are, rather than thinking we have to change them. We have learned how to fight. These habits have changed our relationship from healthy to healthier, from strong to stronger and from close to closer.

Most of us resist change because much of the time the change is accompanied by tension. Fear of change is basic to human nature, even if the changes are positive. Change means venturing into the unfamiliar and unknown. Change can bring embarrassment to us. What if the change turns out to be unhealthy to us and to the relationship? What if my spouse does not like the changes I made? What if I decide to change and I fail?

Change can cause discomfort. This reality came to fruition when, after a number of years of marriage, my wife began to redefine the roles she expected of herself as a wife and mother.

During the first part of our marriage, Elaine fulfilled all of the traditional roles of a wife and mother. She cleaned house, washed the clothes and prepared the meals. This is what her mother did and what my mother did. Elaine felt this was expected of her. Then change began to take place. The change almost derailed our marriage.

I did not like the change. I expected her to do everything my mother had done. I enjoyed it. When she began to change, I thought she was just reacting to those who were advocating women's liberation. I thought taking those assertive training seminars was counterproductive to our relationship. Her assertiveness came across as aggressiveness.

At first, I tried anger as a way to get her to realize her changes were not a good thing. My anger only drove her further into change. Using guilt to change her back was also met with resistance. Despite my attempts, she proceeded to change into what she wanted to be and do. We had to renegotiate the marriage contract in regard to role expectations. For example, I began to assume a larger role in preparing meals and cleaning the house.

For Elaine, the change had to do with her identity as a female and wife. The change threw me off since I was accustomed to her being one kind of person and now she was developing into another.

What helped me most in finally accepting Elaine's revised self-definition was the fact I knew she liked herself better. She was changing into a person she felt was really her. Elaine realized loving and respecting me was tied to loving and respecting herself. It took time and patience on Elaine's part in order for me to realize I would be better off if she was free to develop into a person she liked and wanted to be. I discovered loving me more was connected to loving herself more.

Elaine was changing into a new person, at least to some degree. I realized I needed to love the new person she was becoming. Adjusting to her personality changes took time. It also required help from some good friends and counselors in order for me to realize how my wife's changes would ultimately strengthen our married love.

Change can be received with agitation or as an opportunity to shape the marriage into what both partners want. If you are resisting change, be honest in asking yourself what your marriage would be like today if neither spouse had made any changes. Not all change is good or easy to accept.

Consider there are only three real options when it comes to responding to your spouse when he/she is doing and/or saying something you do not like.

1. Get a divorce. You decide the problems in your marriage are too exasperating and entrenched. Change is not realistic.
2. Wait until your partner changes and in the meantime continue the hurt.
3. Your partner may or may not change throughout the life of your marriage. Hope is found in the third option: **Change your response** to what your spouse does and says. You can only change yourself, and you have to decide what that looks like in your life.

Some people do not respond favorably to the idea that change in themselves and their marriage comes through examining, analyzing and discussing the various marriage issues as discussed in this book. They prefer to approach change with the philosophy, "just do it."

I recall my conversation with J.B. who came to me for counseling. He was having emotional problems that were negatively affecting his happiness and marriage. He was interested in making some changes in himself. After listening to him, I realized the underlying issue was his low self-esteem. I invited him to consider examining his insecurities. He was reluctant, but he consented.

At the beginning of the third session J.B said, "I really don't want to continue all this self-examination. It seems so negative. Spending so much time and energy analyzing doesn't make sense to me." I'm the type of guy who does better by acting myself into changing rather than analyzing. His philosophy was, "Just do it." While this approach can be an effective way to activate your power and bring about change, I offer words of caution.

Just because someone has a good idea or receives a helpful suggestion does not mean he/she has the willpower to carry out the idea or suggestion. The nature of our insecure feelings leaves us with a degree of powerlessness. I have had times when I knew what I wanted to do to make our marriage better and did not do it.

For example, I have heard the advice to fight fair and think about my wife's point of view. Good advice, but wanting to "just do it" does not end up in my doing it. When Elaine insists she is right and I am wrong and when she expresses impatience with me, responding with patience and understanding through positive thinking feels unrealistic. The advice is on target, but my willpower is weak.

After determining the problem in the marriage, it would be wonderful if a counselor could simply tell us what to do or not do and bingo, it would happen. If people would take my advice and do what I tell them to do, I could solve every couple's marital problems in 30 minutes or less. Obviously it is not that easy. It is one thing to tell someone to change his/her attitude and behavior, and it is quite another thing to effectively implement the changes.

Why is it couples have difficulty implementing good advice? It is not because they disagree with the suggestions or do not want to do them. Often it has to do with advice-giving itself. When we were children we got lots of advice from our parents. Usually we complied. Being compliant is a childlike response. Sometimes children follow compliance with defiance.

When adults act out of their compliant child, the results are predictable. They may do the suggestion for awhile, but then either openly (or subtly) resists or simply drifts away from responsible action. Good behavior that is the result of child-like compliance, no matter how well intended, lacks the power and wisdom necessary for sustaining the desired actions.

I recall a time in a share group when a mother asked me for advice. Her adult daughter was doing some things that did not make sense to her as a mother. She said to me, "Don't ask me questions like you usually do. I want to know your opinion. What should I do?" Against my better judgment I told her what I thought she should do. In a few minutes she was mad at me and resisting what I told her.

Rather than giving a prescription for having a healthy marriage, this book has been an invitation into a process for making love the married way. If the "just do it" approach works best for you and you have sufficient power for carrying out the suggestions, then do it. If advice and suggestions are what you want, here is a list that may be helpful to you.

- Don't overreact
- Fight fairly and constructively
- Assume a degree of control of your anger
- Focus on the best in you and your spouse, not the worst
- Don't insist on being right
- Don't be negative; be resilient
- Take responsibility for what is happening rather than blaming your spouse
- Appreciate the other's point of view
- Express your feelings calmly
- Don't attack your spouse's self-esteem
- In an argument, focus on the behavior rather than attack your spouse
- In an argument, look for solutions rather than identifying the culprit
- Be empathetic
- Develop a more positive self-image
- Love unconditionally
- Be patient
- Learn to tolerate criticism
- Don't be defensive
- Do loving things for your spouse each day even if you don't feel like it
- Don't respond to your spouse's criticism with negativity
- Accept your partner's faults
- Take care of yourself
- Practice restraint
- Develop the ability to quiet yourself down
- Don't depend on your spouse for validation, rather self-validate

- Value your partner's needs as highly as you value your own
- Abandon your self-defeating tendencies
- Focus on wanting to change yourself not your spouse.
- Don't make mountains out of molehills
- Know your partner's down cycles and give support in those moments
- Know your spouse's intimacy needs and be determined to meet them
- Express appreciation for and interest in your spouse's strengths, talents and uniqueness
- Reduce your dependency on your spouse to make you feel worthwhile
- Learn to be assertive and let your wants be known
- Learn to stop responding with emotion to your spouse's irritating traits
- Become aware of your irrational and self-limiting beliefs and actions
- Do not let your happiness depend on the feedback from your spouse
- Think before you say something you will regret later
- Don't argue about something you can't change
- Be the first to say, "I'm sorry"
- Each day express an unexpected act of love to your spouse
- When you're in disagreement, attack the problems together. Do not attack each other
- Brag on your partner in front of others
- Avoid sarcasm
- See difficult times as an opportunity for growth
- Remember *how* you say something is just as important as what you say
- Don't take things personally
- Recognize and talk about the changes taking place in you and your spouse that may be causing stress
- Focus on your own imperfections when you start thinking too much about your spouse's imperfections
- Be sensitive when your spouse is tired and stressed and respond accordingly
- Keep a sense of humor

- Learn to soothe yourself and thereby lessen your feelings of anxiety and insecurity
- Re-create your early bonding rituals

Your marriage is a garden. Do not forget the garden is a gift from God. God provides the sun, rain, soil and seed. You and I are called to do what is necessary for the garden to grow and produce the intended fruit. The six habits listed above will help you make certain the seeds of a healthy marriage are planted. God's seed of love will grow and flourish in our marriage as we respond to God's gift with gratitude. The potential of our marriage garden will be realized as we passionately work the soil and faithfully receive the gifts of sun and rain.

View your marriage as a journey, a long journey of faith and love. There will be various stages along this journey. The stages will depend upon a number of factors, such as aging, health, children, work, moving, length of marriage, emotional development, tragedy, etc . . .

All of us would love for the journey to be smooth and straight, but we know this is not reality. In fact, realistic expectations are important as you travel. Expect to make it to your desired destination, but expect there to be some obstacles along the way. In other words, expect the unexpected. There may be a detour or two. Understand the detour is exactly a detour and nothing more. Every detour is temporary and always leads back to the road we want to be on.

Expect there to be potholes. Understand a pothole is a pothole and nothing more. It may or may not cause extensive damage to the marriage. The marriage is always repairable. Expect there to be a wreck or two along the journey. The wreck may cause hurt and pain. More than likely, the wreck will be caused by you, even though your tendency will be to blame it on someone else, such as your spouse. Again, the damage can always be repaired, and you can continue on your journey of faith and love.

You can decide to see failure as an opportunity for growing your married love and take it to a new and renewed level. The detours, potholes and wrecks call for adjustments and changes which can lead to a deeper love and a more enjoyable journey.

Make these six habits part of the hard work, discipline and sacrifice involved in a marriage committed to KISS, keeping in shape systematically.

Marriage is a gift from God. Work passionately at your relationship so you can enjoy every bit of joy wrapped in the gift.

QUESTIONS FOR PERSONAL REFLECTION
AND
DISCUSSION WITH YOUR SPOUSE

KISS 1: How do you feel about going to a counselor? Have there been times in your marriage when you thought about counseling but refrained from mentioning it?

KISS 2: Would you like to attend a marriage workshop/seminar? Why, why not?

KISS 3: Share why a marriage support group would be a good decision for your marriage. Would you be willing to initiate organizing a group?

KISS 4: Share how you would like to grow the spiritual dimension of your marriage.

KISS 5: What steps would you like to take toward making early detection and preventive maintenance a central part of your marriage?

KISS 6: Share the times when you have decided to use a problem as an opportunity for building a stronger marriage.

KISS 7: What changes would you like to make in yourself that you feel would enhance your marriage? What would it take to actualize those changes?

Order Book ($15, includes taxes and shipping)

Schedule Workshop

vbrady4216@sunflower.com